God's Field Hospital

God's Field Hospital

Ignatian Spiritual Exercises Healing Wounds of Life

MICHAEL HANSEN, SJ

Paulist Press
New York / Mahwah, NJ

Cover image by Alexey_Hulsov / Pixabay.com
Cover design by Joe Gallagher
Book design by Lynn Else

Library of Congress Cataloging-in-Publication Data
Names: Hansen, Michael, 1951– author.
Title: God's field hospital: ignatian spiritual exercises healing wounds of life / Michael Hansen, SJ.
Description: New York; Mahwah, NJ: Paulist Press, [2024] | Includes bibliographical references and index. | Summary: "This book presents sixty Ignatian spiritual exercises to heal the wounds of life"—Provided by publisher.
Identifiers: LCCN 2023043031 (print) | LCCN 2023043032 (ebook) | ISBN 9780809156887 (paperback) | ISBN 9780809188536 (ebook)
Subjects: LCSH: Ignatius, of Loyola, Saint, 1491–1556. Exercitia spiritualia. | Spiritual exercises.
Classification: LCC BX2179.L8 H276 2024 (print) | LCC BX2179.L8 (ebook) | DDC 248.3—dc23/eng/20240213
LC record available at https://lccn.loc.gov/2023043031
LC ebook record available at https://lccn.loc.gov/2023043032

ISBN 978-0-8091-5688-7 (paperback)
ISBN 978-0-8091-8853-6 (e-book)

Published by Paulist Press
997 Macarthur Boulevard
Mahwah, New Jersey 07430
www.paulistpress.com

Printed and bound in the
United States of America

Dedication

To the givers of these exercises
and those creating field-hospital churches
on the frontlines of hurt and sorrow.

The Church must be like a field hospital that
cleans and heals wounds.
This is the mission of the Church: The Church heals, it cures.
Sometimes, I speak of the Church as if it were a field hospital.
It's true: there are many, many wounded!

—Pope Francis,
"Homily at Mass in Santa Marta,"
February 5, 2015

Contents

II. Medical Care

III. Intensive Care

Foreword

In August 2013, when I first interviewed Francis, he had been elected pope only a few months, but from the first moments of our meeting, I sensed that he was communicating a very strong and lucid vision of the church and its mission in the world, the fruit of his pastoral and spiritual experience. I recognized in his words the *Spiritual Exercises of St. Ignatius of Loyola*, especially that meditation in which Ignatius invites us to contemplate the wounded world, and the decision of the divine Persons who say to each other, "Let us redeem humanity," which brought forth the incarnation.

The pope said, "I see clearly that the thing the church needs most today is the ability to heal the wounds and to warm the hearts of the faithful, with closeness and proximity. I see the church as a field hospital after battle. It is useless to ask a seriously wounded person if he has high cholesterol and high sugar! One must treat his wounds. Then we can talk about everything else. Heal the wounds, heal the wounds...." The pope also repeated this to the parish priests of Rome on March 6, 2014: "You will do the specialized care, but first you must heal the open wounds." He has repeated this appeal on other occasions as well. These important words resonate today in a broken, divided, and wounded world, and they are full of meaning.

Clearly, however, this work of rescue and salvation does not consider the "wounded" as completely lacking in capacity to react or merely as a dying person. The frequent images Bergoglio draws from the world of health care need to be developed. For the pope, "we cannot cure a sick person if we do not start from what is healthy about him." And that means starting from the positive, from the resources that are still available, from an openness to grace that has not been affected, from health care that is not incurably undermined. In short, ensuring that our freedom and ability to act and react has not been sapped. Francis has great confidence in the positive resources of our humanity.

This confidence always makes me reflect on an event in Francis's life that is connected to his attitude of "care," even in the medical sense: before entering the seminary, Jorge Mario Bergoglio became seriously ill and at the age of twenty-one almost died of a lung infection. In a moment of high fever, he hugged his mother in despair, saying, "Tell me what is happening to me!" He was diagnosed with pneumonia and the presence of three cysts. Because of this, the upper part of his right lung was removed. The convalescence was hard because of the method of draining the fluid that had formed in his lungs. I imagine what it could mean for a young man to feel short of breath, to need immediate care, to need relief. I believe that this, in some way, shaped Pope Francis's great and deep human and spiritual sensitivity.

Michael Hansen's book *God's Field Hospital* is a very important contribution to exercise one's spiritual gaze and feel the healing power of the gospel both in one's own life and in the life of the world. It constitutes an itinerary that personally involves those who undertake it, requiring full personal participation. What one needs to desire and ask in the journey, then, is to feel the healing power of God's grace personally and to be of service to the world as people who help heal wounds.

One of the most heartfelt questions the Pontiff asked the pastors of the church in the interview I gave him was:

"How are we treating God's people?" Even the verb, *treating*, is to be read perhaps in the sense of *care* in the context of a *field hospital*. And *treatment* takes time, for it is realized over time and is open to the future of a healing process. Treatment is not miraculous, instantaneous: it needs a special time. Mercy also requires time. It requires a tension toward the future, without which it is meaningless. There is a process of progressive improvement that must remain open. Every rigid obstacle, every hindrance that precludes a path of improvement is an offense against God's mercy. Then the ministers of the church must take charge of people, accompanying them like the Good Samaritan who washes, cleans, and lifts up his neighbor. This is pure gospel—an exercise in healing sores and wounds. But I believe that the medical gaze is not reserved exclusively for pastors but must also be embodied by each of us. In this sense the book *God's Field Hospital* is an important tool.

To take the path that Michael Hansen proposes is to fulfill what Francis asked for in his Bull of Indiction of the Extraordinary Jubilee of Mercy, *Misericordiae vultus*: "Let us open our eyes and see the misery of the world, the wounds of our brothers and sisters who are denied their dignity, and let us recognize that we are compelled to heed their cry for help! May we reach out to them and support them so they can feel the warmth of our presence, our friendship, and our fraternity!" (no. 15).

This book helps open our eyes to make us willing to open our hands. Like any true spiritual exercise, it is not to be *read* but to be *done*: it proposes exercises, not theoretical meditations. It will not simply nourish our minds, but our very ability to see ourselves and the world. And perhaps it will help those who take the proposed path of working to make our world a better place.

Introduction

I see clearly that the thing the church needs most today is the ability to heal the wounds and to warm the hearts of the faithful, with closeness and, proximity.

I see the church as a field hospital after battle. It is useless to ask a seriously wounded person if he has high cholesterol and high sugar! One must treat his wounds. Then we can talk about everything else. Heal the wounds, heal the wounds… and you must start from the ground up.

—Pope Francis,
"Interview with Antonio Spadaro, SJ,"
America, 2013

Pope Francis imagines the church as a frontline field hospital, a church that is quickly responsive to urgent needs, adaptable to the situation, modular, mobile, safe, and a temporary configuration for greater freedom in mission. It is always near the people where they suffer and are wounded. What might such a flexible church have to offer? What kind of healing is needed on the battlefield of people's lives today? This book responds to these questions with specific exercises based on the *Spiritual Exercises of St. Ignatius* for healing on the frontiers or margins of our life.

This book is not *about* a field hospital. It does not teach or explain; it *is* a field hospital. It offers real treatment by the greatest physician of all, the healing Spirit of God, for those hurt, wounded, or ill, for those who find themselves in the dark, nursing a cold heart, and holding on to a failing life.

Imagining God's Field Hospital

"The church as a field hospital" is a metaphor, a way of speaking that correlate two seemingly unrelated ideas to make the listener see them in a new way. In this case "church" and "field hospital." A metaphor equates these two things directly, visually, and emotionally, as one and the same. It stretches you to imagine the church as a field hospital, as "God's field hospital."

The book presents a fully developed metaphor of a field hospital directory offering healing for specific wounds and illness, both physical and spiritual. In it, there are five broad levels of care: Emergency, Medical, Intensive, Specialist, and Recovery.

There are fifteen departments within them: admissions, emergency, and diagnosis begin at the entrance of the field hospital. Then there are the first responses of health, first aid, and mental health. Following this are the lifesaving modules for critical, surgical, and coronary care. Specialist care is offered in modules for respiratory, orthopedic, and pain management. Finally, there are the short-term wards for physical therapy, rehabilitation, and recovery.

Each department represents the different mobile units, or modules, of a field hospital, a spine and branch of tents linked together into pathways of healing.

Within each department, there are four spiritual exercises. Each individual exercise has a description and a list of symptoms. Each exercise is a means of care for body, mind, and spirit. They are for anyone affected by suffering, illness, or wounds, and it is better to use them in prayer than to explain them. While the structure of these exercises is simple, their purpose is to go deeper and treat the wounds immediately.

Pope Francis explains that "a field hospital church is a place for urgent care…a church that goes forth toward those who are 'wounded,' who are in need of an attentive ear, understanding, forgiveness, and love."[1]

Choosing a Healing Exercise

Choice or desire in Ignatian prayer is paramount, and in a field hospital one needs a specific treatment for a specific wound or illness. Each diagnosis, each healing path, is unique to each person. So, how does one choose the right healing exercise?

Retreat books offer linear programs of prayer. They often have themes with a start and an end, various ways to pray, and reflections by the author. A field hospital of spiritual exercises is completely different. This book is neither linear nor bound by a beginning and an end. The author is invisible. *God's Field Hospital* is more like a piano or a kitchen, to use two metaphors.

THE PIANO AND THE SONG

A piano keyboard has black and white keys, and each are the same in shape and function respectively. *God's Field Hospital* has sixty exercises that are virtually the same in structure, shape, and function. With a piano keyboard, you have an almost infinite number of ways to play and create wonderful music.

In *God's Field Hospital* the variety of exercises is also great. The healing in purpose and effect can be wonderful as well, but healing can only begin by praying the best exercise. So, the one who needs the healing must choose the exercise

1. Pope Francis, *The Name of God Is Mercy: A Conversation with Andrea Tornielli* (New York: Doubleday, 2017), 50.

that meets her or his specific need for healing and will vary for each person. There is no linear program; your healing is your song.

THE KITCHEN AND THE FEAST

Consider the kitchen and all the ingredients and spices in the pantry and fridge. These are the same for every meal, the spices are the same collection of spices, and the protein and vegetables are the same, but how one uses spices, in what proportion and preparation, and how the meat, fish, or vegetables are prepared, provide a great variety of meals. In *God's Field Hospital,* the one in need of healing tastes and chooses exercises respective of their need. Each hunger is different, each want is unique, and each healing meal will be special. Your healing is your feast.

Choice and Desire

How do I choose the best exercise for my healing? There are six good ways to find the best exercise. Each field hospital department is introduced by the titles, descriptions, and symptoms of its four exercises. Furthermore, each exercise has a unique desire, scripture passage, and Spirit of God. All these can be helpful. Choose the one that you feel attracted to in any of the departments. The index at the back of the book contains a full list of symptoms. Your healing is your heart's desire.

What if someone wants to pray several exercises for an extended treatment of a wound or illness? There are two possibilities, the first is to choose the best exercise and then pray the other three exercises in the same department. They are linked deliberately. The second is to choose the two, three, or as many exercises as you like, for a healing pathway.

Please note that there is no single perfect choice, so you cannot really go wrong. Relax and try the one that appears best. If it does not meet your need, choose another. The Spirit will help you.

Flowing with a Healing Exercise

The *Spiritual Exercises of St. Ignatius* are highly structured, guided, and focused. They are *structured* using a set of regular steps, *guided* by the desire of the exercise, and *focused* on the relationship between God and the receiver, the one praying the exercise.[2]

The structure of the exercises is like a trellis for a climbing plant. It supports the plant as it grows, but it does not affect the direction, the speed of growth, or the fruit of that plant.

There are two types of exercises in *God's Field Hospital*. Forty-four exercises are for direct healing, and there are sixteen exercises for healing discernment that are marked with an asterisk in the table of contents. The direct healing exercises focus on a particular illness, wound, or need. The exercises for healing discernment focus on life-giving choices that affect the whole person—the healing direction to move in, usually with greater freedom.

An essential dynamic of the discernment exercises for healing is the understanding and naming of a *contrary* experience. A contrary experience has three features that make it valuable. First, each contrary experience reveals much about the original experience, for example, love and rejection. Second, contrary experiences are not just opposites, they move in contrary directions, for example, toward greater love or deeper rejection. Third, contrary experiences are very personal, rooted in my memories and life journey, for example, my experience of being loved or rejected. Naming a contrary

2. The original five-step structure of the Ignatian *Spiritual Exercises* are Preparation, Introductory Prayer, Desire, Prayer, and Conversation.

experience reveals the best way forward in my life at any particular time when healing is needed.

In sum, one may move away from God, into darkness and deeper alienation from the Healer, or one may move toward God, into greater intimacy and peace in the Healer.

The core moment of the direct healing exercise is "breathing" in the Spirit. The core moment for the exercises for healing discernment is "resting" in the Spirit. Breathing and resting are simple, deep, healing ways to join with the Spirit of God. Each way of praying has its own dynamic and flow.

Receiving a Healing Exercise

In each of the field hospital exercises, the receiver is invited to meet God directly. This way of meeting God through a structured spiritual exercise was developed by St. Ignatius of Loyola more than five hundred years ago. This form of prayer has helped many people during times of feast and famine, peace and plague, inside and outside the church. It is always offered freely, humbly, without coercion.

These *spiritual exercises* always draw upon the life experience of the receiver. Without judgment, they honor a person's entire life journey. No one else can intrude, not the giver of an exercise, an expert, a holier person, or anyone else. The exercise simply holds God and the receiver; what happens is up to them both and is a key element of Ignatian spirituality.

Ignatian spirituality includes prayer forms that use the imagination, memory, image, and symbol. The exercises within this book also do that. Another Ignatian element is the use of the senses and body, like holding, touching, breathing, and feeling. The last Ignatian element is prayer or contemplation that leads to action, love, or gratitude expressed in deed. Each exercise ends by reaching out to others.

There are some surprising advantages to this form of prayer. First, the receiver needs no preparation, just the generosity to pray the exercise. There is no training, level of faith, or knowledge of church necessary. These exercises are for everyone of goodwill.

To really know how to choose, flow with, and receive an exercise, go, and pray, receive the healing first. Then the above descriptions will be well revealed in your own prayer experience.

Ministry and Mission

The ministers of the Gospel must be people who can warm the hearts of the people, who walk through the dark night with them, who know how to dialogue and to descend themselves into their people's night, into the darkness, but without getting lost.

—Pope Francis,
"Interview with Antonio Spadaro, SJ,"
America, 2013

Pope Francis, here, is describing health workers in God's field hospital. He is also naming the healing that provides warmth, support, and conversation to someone living in the dark. This intimate, caring presence almost defines the mission of the church. Pope Francis exclaims:

> So many people need their wounds healed! This is the mission of the Church: to heal the wounds of the heart, to open doors, to free people, to say that God is good, God forgives all, God is the Father, God is affectionate, God always waits for us. (Homily at Mass in Santa Marta, February 5, 2015)

I

Emergency Care

Admissions

We begin at the entrance. While people seeking help at a field hospital can come alone, more often they are supported by paramedics, coworkers, family, or friends. Even so, it can be a frightening experience. A warm welcome, a competent hand, and reassuring knowledge will begin healing.

Exercise 1: Carried. The sick or wounded person is carried both physically and emotionally to the field hospital by their helpers. The Spirit of Friendship is active in this loving support. This first exercise is for those who need to be carried to a field hospital.

Exercise 2: Welcomed. Admissions in God's field hospital welcomes both the body and the spirit. The welcome is an invitation into a healing relationship with both the health-care workers and the God who heals. The Spirit of Welcome lives in this department. This second exercise is for everyone who needs a warm welcome into healing.

Exercise 3: Accompanied. People in pain need someone to accompany them throughout the journey of treatment and healing. This is a vital role for nursing, family, and carers. The Spirit of Accompaniment will be present throughout recovery. Exercise 3 is for those who need company for their unknown future.

Exercise 4: Accepted. What if the patient is not a believer, or churchgoer, or sees themselves as unworthy, even undeserving? Admissions needs be free of even a hint of discrimination, accepting anybody. The Spirit of Inclusion guards the admissions. This fourth exercise is about unconditional acceptance.

Symptoms for Admission

Exercise 1. I need help and healing now. I cannot wait. I cannot reach help alone. I need support for this difficult journey. I feel powerless. I desire to be carried to the field hospital.

Exercise 2. I am hurt and wounded. I feel abandoned. If I come to the field hospital, will I be well received? Even while hurting, I have my dignity. I desire to be welcomed to treatment.

Exercise 3. I feel alone and anxious. I feel afraid because the future is unknown. I need a friend. Who will walk with me without judgment? I desire to be accompanied in my healing.

Exercise 4. I am afraid of rejection. Given my need for healing, the last thing I want is discrimination. I need to be respected as I am, without prejudice. I desire to be unconditionally accepted.

Exercise 1: **Carried**

Touch •
I touch the heart of friendship.

I hold two cups, one full of water, one empty. Each cup is a friend. I pour water, life, from one cup into the other. When I pour it back again, the action becomes a symbol of friendship where each one gives and receives from the other. I repeat this as desired.

I recall a story of someone who was a friend to me in desperate times. If praying alone, I hold that memory. If I am praying in a group, I share it with them, listening in turn to their stories, feeling touched by the Spirit of Friendship.

Desire •
I desire to be carried to hospital.

I slowly and prayerfully read the scripture text below:

> Some men came, carrying a paralyzed man on a bed. They were trying to bring him in and lay him before Jesus; but finding no way to bring him in because of the crowd, they went up on the roof and let him down with his bed through the tiles into the middle of the crowd in front of Jesus.... Jesus said, "I say to you, stand up and take your bed and go to your home." Immediately he stood up before them, took what he had been lying on, and went to his home, glorifying God. Amazement seized all of them, and they glorified God and were filled with awe, saying, "We have seen strange things today." (Luke 5:18–19, 24–26)

I name all the people I want to carry me to healing and help.

I ask the Spirit of Friendship to help me be carried by a friend when I am in critical need. When life-threatening illness strips away ordinary supports, a friendship can be lifesaving.

Breathe •

I breathe in the Spirit of Friendship.

I imagine and feel the Spirit of Friendship unfurling in me, releasing the love and practical help that reaches out in friendship. I breathe it in deeply, wait, and then breathe it out into those who can carry me to urgent healing.

I repeat as desired—breathing, hoping, befriending…

If I belong to a group, we breathe this Spirit in and out together.

Reach Out •

I reach out to those of like mind and heart.

I conclude in thanks, considering two questions. First, if possible, how might I reconnect with the one who carried me so well? Second, to whom and how do I pass on this exercise? Who needs someone to carry them now?

Exercise 2: **Welcomed**

Touch •

I touch the heart of welcome.

I prepare a cup of tea, coffee, cool water, or some drink that I would normally offer to guests to make them feel at home. I hold it, remembering all the times and ways that I have been warmly welcomed.

I recall a story of being really welcomed when I needed it. If praying alone, I hold that memory. If I am praying in a group, I share it with them, listening in turn to their stories, feeling touched by the Spirit of Welcome.

Desire •

I desire to be welcomed.

I slowly and prayerfully read the scripture text below:

> If there is famine in the land, if there is plague, blight, mildew, locust, or caterpillar; if their enemy besieges them; whatever plague, whatever sickness there is; whatever prayer, whatever plea there is from any individual or from all your people Israel, all knowing the afflictions of their own hearts so that they stretch out their hands toward this house; then hear in heaven your dwelling place, forgive, act, and render to all whose hearts you know. (1 Kgs 8:37–40)

I name all the people, places, and events that I wish would welcome me.

I ask the Spirit of Welcome to become a person ready and open to a warm welcome, to generous hospitality, and to being cared for. I ask for the gift to be a good receiver when I am sick, afraid, helpless, afflicted, or one of the least in my community.

Breathe •

I breathe in the Spirit of Welcome.

Imagine and feel the Spirit of Welcome breathing the gift of being a good and gracious receiver into me. I appreciate this, as I am more comfortable being a giver.

I breathe it in deeply, wait, and then breathe it out to warm all those who have, and all those who may, welcome me in the future, especially when I have an anxious heart, feel alone, or need healing.

I repeat as desired—breathing, welcomed, warmed…

If I belong to a group, we breathe this Spirit in and out together.

Reach Out •

I reach out to those of like mind and heart.

I conclude in thanks, considering two questions. First, if possible, how might I reconnect with the one who really welcomed me? Second, to whom and how do I pass on this exercise? Who urgently needs a warm welcome now?

Exercise 3: **Accompanied**

Touch •
I touch the heart of accompanying.

I create and hold two interlocked rings, like key rings, symbols of journeying with a person in need, practically, emotionally, and spiritually.

I recall a story of being accompanied at a critical time in my life. If praying alone I hold that memory. If I am praying in a group, I share it with them, feeling touched by the Spirit of Accompaniment.

Desire •
I desire to be accompanied.

I slowly and prayerfully read the scripture text below:

> We were gentle among you, like a nurse tenderly caring for her own children. So deeply do we care for you that we are determined to share with you not only the gospel of God but also our own selves, because you have become very dear to us. (1 Thess 2:5–8)

I name all the people whom I want to accompany me.

I ask the Spirit of Accompaniment for the gift accompaniment when I am suffering and journeying alone, or when I need emergency care and support.

Breathe •

I breathe in the Spirit of Accompaniment.

I imagine the Spirit of Accompaniment breathing the need for nursing into me. I breathe it in deeply, wait, and then breathe it out into myself and into those who could also accompany people suffering illness, isolation, alienation, rejection, or dismissal.

I repeat as desired—breathing, accepting, ready for accompaniment...

If I belong to a group, we breathe this Spirit in and out together.

Reach Out •

I reach out to those of like mind and heart.

I conclude in thanks, considering two questions. First, if possible, how might I reconnect with the one who accompanied me so well? Second, to whom and how do I pass on this exercise? Who can help to accompany me?

Exercise 4: **Accepted**

Touch •

I touch the heart of being inclusive.

I hold three leather cords, or ribbons, or pieces of string. I weave them into one cord, in a triple plait, considering, as I do so, that including an extra cord into the first two makes each of them so much stronger, and more beautiful, and a symbol of inclusivity.

I recall a story of being really included when I felt like an outsider. If praying alone, I hold that memory. If I am praying in a group, I share it with them, listening in turn to their stories, feeling touched by the Spirit of Unconditional Acceptance.

Desire •

I desire to be accepted.

I slowly and prayerfully read the scripture text below:

> As many of you as were baptized into Christ have clothed yourselves with Christ. There is no longer Jew or Greek, there is no longer slave or free, there is no longer male and female; for all of you are one in Christ Jesus. For freedom Christ has set us free. Stand firm, therefore, and do not submit again to a yoke of slavery. For in Christ Jesus neither circumcision nor uncircumcision counts for anything; the only thing that counts is faith working through love. (Gal 3:27–28; 5:1, 6)

I name all the people I want to accept, respect and love me with practical help.

I ask the Spirit for the gift of being accepted when I am unnoticed or forgotten, living on the edges, and excluded from urgent health care.

Breathe •

I breathe in the Spirit of Acceptance.

I imagine and feel the Spirit of Unconditional Acceptance breathing greater freedom and inclusive love into me and those who would accept me.

I breathe them in deeply, wait, and then breathe them out into those ready to accept me.

I repeat as desired—breathing, accepted, included...

If I belong to a group, we breathe this Spirit in and out together.

Reach Out •

I reach out to those of like mind and heart.

I conclude in thanks, considering two questions. First, if possible, how might I reconnect with the one who made me feel so included? Second, to whom and how do I pass on this exercise? Who needs unconditional acceptance?

Emergency

The emergency or casualty department preserves life by cleaning wounds, keeping the heart beating, setting broken bones, and providing urgently needed medication. It is here that patients are helped to survive. God's field hospital is ready to receive those with wounds of the body and/or wounds of the spirit.

Exercise 5: Triage of Wounds. Wounds may be fresh or old and still festering. New wounds are treated immediately. Old wounds need to be cleaned. The past cannot be changed, but in God's field hospital, their meaning can be transformed. The Spirit of Health will do this. The fifth exercise is for those who need recovery and peace.

Exercise 6: Trauma Protection. Field hospital patients are often traumatized. God's field hospital is at the front lines of disaster areas in the aftermath of violence or pandemics. The Spirit of Protection covers God's casualty department. The sixth exercise is for those who need help after trauma.

*Exercise 7: Survival Strength.** Through serious ill health, one is brought low, often suddenly, and the strength to cope, the ability to heal oneself, is lost. Finding a heart roiled in confusion and a fragility that sweeps past sureties aside is very common. The Spirit of Strength is needed. The seventh exercise is for those who need the strength to survive.

Exercise 8: Back to Life. God's emergency department is ready for those experiencing death in some form. It is also ready for a faith that has lost hope, is bleeding or has been broken by abuse, or is simply a heart dying for new life. The Spirit of New Life revives us. The eighth exercise is for those who need a death turned into life.

Symptoms of an Emergency

Exercise 5. I need my wounds cleaned and closed. I am in danger of them getting worse. I feel sapped of energy and drained of hope. I desire healing and peace of mind.

Exercise 6. I need trauma protection. I am stunned, stopped, brought low by events and circumstance. I am numb and in shock; my body and mind are shutting down. I desire protection.

Exercise 7. I need strength to survive. I am knocked down but not out. My life is like riding a bucking raft twisting down a wild river. I am just holding on, weakened by illness. I desire inner strength.

Exercise 8. I feel like death. It is hard to remember when I was last well. Now I am dying, wrapped in a shroud of darkness and illness, entombed and powerless. I desire to be raised back to life.

Exercise 5: **Triage of Wounds**

Touch •
I touch the heart of healing.

I trace a cross on my forehead and on the site of my illness. I own how frightening it is to be ill, facing an uncertain future, yearning for healing and peace of mind.

Desire •
I desire healing.

I slowly and prayerfully read the gospel story of Thomas and the risen Jesus:

> The doors of the house were locked for fear of the Jews, Jesus came and stood among his disciples and said, "Peace be with you." After he said this, he showed them his hands and his side. Then the disciples rejoiced when they saw the Lord. But Thomas was not with them when Jesus came. So, the other disciples told him, "We have seen the Lord." But he said to them, "Unless I see the mark of the nails in his hands and put my finger in the mark of the nails and my hand in his side, I will not believe." Later his disciples were again in the house, and Thomas was with them. Although the doors were shut, Jesus came and stood among them and said, "Peace be with you." Then he said to Thomas, "Put your finger here and see my hands. Reach out your hand and put it in my side. Do not doubt but believe." Thomas answered him, "My Lord and my God!" (John 20:19–29)

Jesus invites Thomas to touch his healed wounds. In a triage of heart and faith, Jesus touches the wounds in Thomas's heart and Thomas experiences healing and proclaims faith. So, I take the place of Thomas, for a time, feeling my way into relationship with Jesus, checking symptoms, wound to wound, healing to healing.

I name the healing of body, mind, and heart that I desire.

I ask Jesus for peace of mind, to be touched and healed by him, to touch his healed wounds and find hope for myself. I ask him to walk with me on the long and bumpy road to health and the mystery of how that healing may be.

Breathe •

I breathe in the Spirit of Health.

I imagine the Spirit of Health breathing healing, faith, and peace into me.

I breathe them in deeply, pause, then breathe them out into my wounds and hurt.

I repeat as desired—breathing, healing, peaceful....

If I belong to a group in need of healing, we breathe this Spirit in and out together.

Reach Out •

I reach out to those of like mind and heart.

I conclude in thanks, considering two questions. First, do I wish to invite Jesus to walk this journey with me? Second, to whom and how do I pass on this exercise? Who urgently needs healing, and a little faith and peace of mind now?

Exercise 6: **Trauma Protection**

Touch •
I touch the heart of protection.

I take a nut, a symbol of production, considering how its hard shell protects the nut as it grows, waiting for the time when the nut is ready for freedom and seeding new life.

I recall a story of being protected when I needed it. If praying alone, I hold that memory. If I am praying in a group, I share it with them, listening in turn to their stories, feeling touched by the Spirit of Protection.

Desire •
I desire protection.

I slowly and prayerfully read the scripture text below:

> You who live in the shelter of the Most High, who abide in the shadow of the Almighty, will say to the LORD, "My refuge and my fortress; my God, in whom I trust." For he will cover you with his pinions, and under his wings you will find refuge; his faithfulness is a shield and protection. You will not fear the terror of the night, or the arrow that flies by day, or the pestilence that stalks in darkness, or the destruction that wastes at noonday. Those who love me, I will deliver; I will protect those who know my name. When they call to me, I will answer them; I will be with them in trouble, I will rescue them and honor them. With long life I will satisfy them and show them my salvation. (Ps 91:1–6, 14–16)

I name everything I wish protection from, and all those I wish to protect.

I ask the Spirit for protection from that which threatens my life now, whatever it's form, for the Spirit's wings to cover and shelter me. I ask that my trembling heart become a seed of new life after the destruction threatening me has passed.

Breathe •

I breathe in the Spirit of Protection.

I imagine and feel the Spirit breathing protection and safety into me.

I breathe them in deeply, wait, and then breathe them out to flow through my vulnerability and troubles, making me safe.

I repeat as desired—breathing, protected, safe....

If I belong to a protecting group, we breathe this Spirit in and out together.

Reach Out •

I reach out to those of like mind and heart.

I conclude in thanks, considering two questions. First, if possible, how might I reconnect with the one who protected me? Second, to whom and how do I pass on this exercise? Who urgently needs protection now?

Exercise 7: **Strength to Survive***

Touch •

I touch the heart of spiritual strength.

I hold an object that symbolizes spiritual strength for me.

I recall a story of receiving spiritual strength when I really needed it. If praying alone, I hold that memory. If I am praying in a group, I share it with them, listening in turn to their stories, feeling touched by the Spirit of Strength.

Desire •

I desire inner strength.

I consider three things, taking a few minutes to explore each. I ask myself:

> Where is the spiritual strength present in my life?
>
> Where is the spiritual strength absent in my life?
>
> What, for me, is the contrary or opposite of this strength?

I ask the Spirit to strengthen me, to enhearten and teach me how to steer through the dark waters of my life when I find myself in danger of capsizing.

Choose •

Today, I choose the way of strength.

I slowly and prayerfully read the scripture text below:

> I love you, O LORD, my strength. The Lord is my rock, my fortress, and my deliverer, my God, my rock in whom I take refuge, my shield, and the horn of my salvation, my stronghold. The cords of death encompassed me; the torrents of hell assailed me; the cords of the house of the dead entangled me; the snares of death

confronted me. In my distress I called upon the LORD; to my God I cried for help. My cry to him reached his ears. He reached down from on high, he took me; he drew me out of mighty waters. He brought me out into a broad place; he delivered me, because he delighted in me. (Ps 18:1–2, 6, 16–17, 19)

I choose, in three thoughtful steps, the direction I wish to take:

I choose the strengthening way, led by the good spirit, to the broad place of God.

I reject the disheartening way, the snares of discouragement, led by the bad spirit.

I turn and walk in the contrary direction, from being demoralized, to being strong, to being full of delight.

Rest •

I rest in the Spirit of Strength.

I imagine the Spirit addresses me by name, saying, "Welcome to my stronghold."

So, I rest now, and reflectively through the whole day, in the Spirit's gentle strength, protection, and delight. I feel delivered, relieved, and stronger in spirit.

If I belong to a group seeking spiritual strength, we rest in this Spirit together.

Reach Out •

I reach out to those of like mind and heart.

I conclude in thanks, considering two questions. First, if possible, how might I reconnect with the one who made me stronger? Second, to whom and how do I pass on this exercise? Who urgently needs spiritual strengthening now?

Exercise 8: **Back to Life**

Touch •

I touch the heart of life after death.

I go to a plant nursery where seeds are sold, or somewhere similar. I look at all the packets of flower seeds with pictures of their blooming. A flower has a visible heart. I choose one that symbolizes the life I need now in my dying.

My "death" or dying could be some true part of myself that I have lost, a great dream or desire I once had, now dead and buried; or the child within me is dying and in need of a life; or a threatening illness or change that seems to have killed a future I hoped for.

I recall a story of being raised back to life and the one who lifted me up. If praying alone, I hold that memory. If I am praying in a group, I share it with them, listening in turn to their stories, feeling touched by the Spirit of Life.

Desire •

I desire to come back to life.

I slowly and prayerfully read the scripture text below:

> Jairus fell at Jesus' feet and begged him repeatedly, "My little daughter is at the point of death. Come and lay your hands on her, so that she may be made well, and live." So Jesus went with him. On the way some people came to say, "Your daughter is dead. Why trouble the teacher any further?" But overhearing what they said, Jesus said to the leader of the synagogue, "Do not fear, only believe." When they came to the house, Jesus took the girl by the hand and said to her, "Talitha cum," which means, "Little girl, get up!" And immediately the girl got up and began to walk about. (Mark 5:22–42)

I name the dead part of me, or my life, that I desire to be lifted up, to be enlivened.

I ask the Spirit to be whole again, to be raised up, and to have a blossoming future.

Breathe •

I breathe in the Spirit of New Life.

I imagine the Spirit addressing me by name, saying, "Do not fear, only believe. Rise!"

I imagine and feel the Spirit breathing new life and hope into me. I breathe them in deeply, wait, and then breathe them out into my dead or dying self, and into all those who, both grieving and weary, feel any new life to be impossible.

I repeat as desired—breathing, rising, wholly alive....

If I belong to a group desiring new life, we breathe this Spirit in and out together.

Reach Out •

I reach out to those of like mind and heart.

I conclude in thanks, considering two questions. First, if possible, how might I reconnect with the person who raised me up? Second, to whom and how do I pass on this exercise? Who urgently needs to be raised back to life?

Diagnosis

In God's casualty department, symptoms are noted; illnesses, disease, and wounds are diagnosed; and a lifeline of action, drugs, or equipment is provided. Here, the body is protected from further harm and the spirit revived.

Exercise 9: Good Diagnosis. Portable X-rays, ultrasounds, and radiology have found their way into field hospitals. With them, specialists can see the hurt beneath the surface. They also listen to the patient describe their pain. The Spirit of Discernment listens, names, identifies, reveals, and clarifies the illness. Exercise 9 is for a good diagnosis.

Exercise 10: Compassionate Touch. Nurses—gentle, selfless healers—treat their patients with compassion. God's field hospital is a place where a hard heart, crippling memories, a dark past, or despair can be healed. The Spirit of Compassion frees and leads the way. Exercise 10 is for those needing to be met and treated with compassion.

Exercise 11: Catching Lifelines. As well as care for the body, care for the soul is offered in God's emergency department. Diagnosing a spiritual illness, providing a lifeline from the effects of evil or injustice, and giving protection to a soul under assault—all this is done by the Spirit of Rescue. Exercise 11 is for those who need safety.

Exercise 12: Tracing Love. While casualty is a physical place, it can also be a spiritual or sacred place—the place of the heart, the place of a dying soul parched for life. It is, despite all the activity and machines, a place of love and hope. The Spirit of Love flows through every act. Exercise 12 is for those who need to be loved.

Symptoms for Diagnosis

Exercise 9. I need a good diagnosis. I need to know what is wrong with me. I cannot wait. I need help to disentangle my symptoms and feelings. I need good healing.

Exercise 10. I need compassionate hands. I yearn to have the muscles of fear and anxiety loosened, to be helped back up. I desire compassionate care.

Exercise 11. I need to be rescued. Where are my lifelines? I am in a dangerous place, in perilous circumstances, in deadly relationships, sinking beneath the waves. I desire safety.

Exercise 12. I need love. I feel loveless and rejected, counted as nothing, walking amid the fires of personal destruction. I need to be held precious. I desire to be loved.

Exercise 9: **Good Diagnosis**

Touch •

I touch the heart of diagnosis.

I hold some medicine, new or old, in my hand. I consider how access to doctors, health care, medicine, and sanitation is a basic human right—the more so during a pandemic. I remember the times I have urgently needed health care and how dire it would have been without it. I open myself to diagnosis by the Spirit of Discernment.

I recall a story of being diagnosed when I was quite ill but did not know what was wrong with me. I remember imagining the worst and then my relief. If praying alone, I hold that memory. If I am praying in a group, I share it with them, listening in turn to their stories, feeling touched by the Spirit of Discernment.

Desire •

I desire diagnosis.

I slowly and prayerfully read the scripture text below:

> Honor physicians for their services, for the Lord created them; for their gift of healing comes from the Most High. The Lord created medicines out of the earth, and the sensible will not despise them. By them the physician heals and takes away pain; the pharmacist makes a mixture from them. God's works will never be finished; and from him health spreads over all the earth. My child, when you are ill, do not delay, but pray to the Lord, and he will heal you. Then give the physician his place, for the Lord created him; do not let him leave you, for you need him. There may come a time when recovery lies in the hands of physicians, for they too pray to the Lord that he grants them success in diagnosis and in healing, for the sake of preserving life. (Sir 38:1–14)

I name the symptoms I wish to be diagnosed.

I ask the Spirit for the diagnosis, medicine, and health care I need, including spiritual health.

Breathe •

I breathe in the Spirit of Discernment.

I imagine and feel the Spirit of Discernment breathing diagnosis, understanding, and the confidence of healing into me.

I breathe them in deeply, wait, and then breathe them out to flow through my ill health.

I repeat as desired—breathing, diagnosed, seeing myself become healthy....

If I belong to a group seeking diagnosis, we breathe this Spirit in and out together.

Reach Out •

I reach out to those of like mind and heart.

I conclude in thanks, considering two questions. First, if possible, how might I reconnect with the person who diagnosed me at a critical time? Second, to whom and how do I pass on this exercise? Who urgently needs diagnosis now?

Exercise 10: **Compassionate Touch**

Touch •

I touch the heart of compassion.

I massage my hands with an aromatic oil or healing ointment, considering how both are used for healing. I smell them and feel the Spirit of Compassion enter me.

I recall a story of receiving compassion when I needed it. If praying alone, I hold that memory. If I am praying in a group, I share it with them, listening in turn to their stories, feeling touched by the Spirit of Compassion.

Desire •

I desire compassionate help.

I slowly and prayerfully read the scripture text below:

> Jesus said, "A man was going to Jericho, and fell into the hands of robbers, who stripped him, beat him, leaving him half dead. Now by chance a priest was on that road; and when he saw him, he passed on the other side. Likewise, a Levite. But a Samaritan, when he saw him, was moved with compassion. He went to him and bandaged his wounds, having poured oil and wine on them. Then he put him on his own animal, brought him to an inn, and took care of him. Which of these three was a neighbour to the man who fell into the hands of the robbers?" The listener said, "The one who showed him mercy." Jesus said to him, "Go and do likewise." (Luke 10:30–37)

I name all the ways I wish to be treated with compassion.

I ask the Spirit for the gift of compassion when I am wounded, abandoned, and need long term care.

Breathe •

I breathe in the Spirit of Compassion.

I imagine and feel the Spirit of Compassion breathing loving kindness into me.

I breathe it in deeply, wait, and then breathe it out into the suffering, violence, wounds, and abandonment I have experienced.

I repeat as desired—breathing, touched compassionately, cared for....

If I belong to a group desiring to receive compassion, we breathe this Spirit together.

Reach Out •

I reach out to those of like mind and heart.

I conclude in thanks, considering two questions. First, if possible, can I reconnect with the person who showed compassion toward me? Second, to whom and how do I pass on this exercise? Who needs gentle, active compassion?

Exercise 11: **Catching Lifelines**

Touch •

I touch the heart of being saved.

I take up a short piece of string, yarn, or cord, seeing in it a symbol of a lifeline.

I hold one end, that is me, and the other end is the Spirit who keeps me safe. I ponder the safety, sustaining life, and unbreakable strength of that connection.

I recall a story of being rescued, given a lifeline, by God or another, when I really needed rescuing. If praying alone I hold that memory. If I am praying in a group, I share it with them, listening in turn to their stories, feeling touched by the Spirit of Life.

Desire •

I desire to be rescued.

I slowly and prayerfully read the scripture text below:

> Save me, O God, for the waters have come up to my neck. I sink in deep mire, where there is no foothold; I have come into deep waters, and the flood sweeps over me. I am weary with my crying; my throat is parched. My eyes grow dim with waiting for my God. I have become a stranger to my kindred, an alien to my mother's children. But as for me, my prayer is to you, O LORD....O God, in the abundance of your steadfast love, answer me. With your faithful help rescue me....I am lowly and in pain; let your salvation, O God, protect me. (Ps 69)

I name all the things from which I wish to be rescued.

I ask the Spirit for safety, for safe keeping, for a lifeline of help, that will never let me go in these precarious and dangerous times.

Breathe •

I breathe in the Spirit of Rescue.

I imagine and feel the Spirit of Rescue breathing into me the surety of rescue, protection, and security.

I breathe it in deeply, wait, and then breathe it out into every crevice of fear, mire of anxiety, flood of tears and cry for help within me. I will imagine both the Spirit's direct help and indirect help through others who can be a lifeline for me.

I repeat as desired—breathing, safe, secure....

If I belong to a group seeking a lifeline, we breathe this Spirit in and out together.

Reach Out •

I reach out to those of like mind and heart.

I conclude in thanks, considering two questions. First, if possible, how might I reconnect with the one who kept me safe? Second, to whom and how do I pass on this exercise? Who urgently needs a lifeline now?

Exercise 12: **Tracing Love**

Touch •

I touch the heart of love.

I hold a cross. I trace and feel the figure of Jesus on it, considering his life-giving love.

I touch his wounds and feel the touch of the loving Spirit on mine.

I remember a small story of someone loving me as I am, when I really needed it. If praying alone I hold that memory. If I am praying in a group, I share it with them, listening in turn to their stories, feeling touched by the Spirit of Love.

Desire •

I desire to be loved.

I slowly and prayerfully read the scripture text below:

> Now says the Lord, he who created you, O Jacob, he who formed you, O Israel: Do not fear, for I have redeemed you; I have called you by name, you are mine. When you pass through the waters, I will be with you; and through the rivers, they shall not overwhelm you; when you walk through fire you shall not be burned, and the flame shall not consume you. For I am the LORD your God, the Holy One of Israel, your Savior. Because you are precious in my sight, and honoured, and I love you. (Isa 43:1–4)

I name all those I wish to love and open myself to all those would love me.

I ask the Spirit to be loved and loving, even in the bleak times when love can be denied in the face of fear, deadly circumstances, or consuming events.

Breathe •
I breathe in the Spirit of Love.

I imagine the Spirit addressing me by name, saying, "You are precious to me, honored in my sight, and I love you."

I imagine the Spirit breathing love into me—the love of Jesus, who died to defeat death, the love of others, the love of creation, and even a healthy love of myself.

I breathe it in deeply, wait, and then breathe it out to fill all my relationships with love and affection, and to flow into those who have been denied love, or live a loveless life.

I repeat as desired—breathing, loved, loving....

If I belong to a group, seeking Jesus's love, we breathe this Spirit in and out together.

Reach Out •
I reach out to those of like mind and heart.

I conclude in thanks, considering two questions. First, if possible, how might I reconnect with the person who loved me when I most needed it? Second, to whom and how do I pass on this exercise.

II

Medical Care

First-Aid Care

First aid in a field hospital may be the only care some need, while for others it may help until the paramedics arrive to take them to a larger, established hospital. First aid will vary based on the specific crisis or need.

Exercise 13: Shelter. Before receiving aid, one must first remove the wounded from immediate danger. The guarded perimeter of a field hospital is a place of safety just behind the front lines. The sheltering Spirit watches over it. Exercise 13 is for those who need the enfolding wings of God to protect them while first aid is provided.

*Exercise 14: Revival.** The first and second steps check for blocked airways and to enable breathing. The Spirit of Revival will help. Exercise 14 is for those who, in one way or another, are struggling to breathe.

Exercise 15. Understanding. The third step is ensuring circulation. It is about the heart and the pulse of life. It is a complex, interdependent relationship of vessels, organs, heart, and brain. Knowledge and experience are needed. The Spirit of Understanding will provide needed wisdom. Exercise 15 is for those whose heart is laboring.

Exercise 16. Respect. After the "ABC"—airways-breathing-circulation—of first aid, the next step is to calm the fearful panic, to hold and comfort the patient. The Spirit of Respect will be present. Exercise 16 is for those who need encouragement to heal.

Symptoms for First Aid

Exercise 13. I need a safe shelter. I am in danger from the storm that threatens me, from the waves that crash against my present needs. I feel really exposed. I desire a strong shelter.

Exercise 14. I need to be revived. I am at risk of dying in my heart—emotionally and spiritually. I need to be filled with loving consolation. I desire life in the face of desolation.

Exercise 15. I need to understand. I have no clarity about the peril I am in. Everything seems too complicated. I desire the wisdom to understand my heart and stay alive.

Exercise 16. I need to be respected. I need to know, even in the face of dreadful illness or wounds, that all will be well in time. I desire encouragement. I need to be respected as I am now.

Exercise 13: **Shelter**

Touch •
I touch the heart of shelter.

I hold a large hat, one I would wear to shelter from the rain or the sun. I consider how shelter is a basic human right. I imagine various kinds of shelters, from a sheltering home to shelter from natural disasters and disease, from wars and conflict to domestic violence. I consider what it would be like without shelter in these situations.

I recall a story of being without shelter and a person who gave me shelter when I was desperate for it. If praying alone, I hold that memory. If I am praying in a group, I share it with them, listening in turn to their stories, feeling touched by the Spirit of Shelter.

Desire •
I desire shelter.

I slowly and prayerfully read the scripture text below:

> The wicked drive away the donkey of the orphan; they take the widow's ox for a pledge. They thrust the needy off the road; the poor of the earth all hide themselves. They lie all night naked, without clothing, and have no covering in the cold. They are wet with the rain of the mountains, and cling to the rock for want of shelter. (Job 24:3–8)

I name all the things from which I need sheltering.
I ask the Spirit for the shelter and protection I need.

Breathe •

I breathe the Spirit of Shelter.

I imagine the Spirit addressing me by name, saying, "Hold firm, take heart. I will shelter you in all your troubles."

I imagine and feel the Spirit sheltering me, breathing steadfastness into me.

I breathe it in deeply, wait, and then breathe it out through my need for a lighthouse in the storm and out into those naked and wet at night for want of shelter.

I repeat as desired—breathing, sheltered, resolute....

If I belong to a group needing shelter, we breathe this Spirit in and out together.

Reach Out •

I reach out to those of like mind and heart.

I conclude in thanks, considering two questions. First, if possible, how might I reconnect with the person who gave me shelter? Second, to whom and how do I pass on this exercise? Who urgently needs shelter now?

Exercise 14: **Revival***

Touch •

I touch the heart of spiritual revival.

I find and hold an object that symbolizes for me the gift of spiritual revival—that interior joy, light, and love from God that revives me in the face of desolation.

I recall a story of being revived when I was desolate, in spirit and emotions. If praying alone, I hold that memory. If I am praying in a group, I share it with them, listening in turn to their stories, feeling touched by the Spirit of Revival.

Desire •

I desire revival.

I consider three things, taking a few minutes to explore each of them. I ask myself:

What revives and consoles me in my life?

What chokes the life from me and causes me to feel desolate?

What, for me, is the contrary or opposite of revival?

I ask the Spirit for the gift of revival, for greater hope, love, and faith, when I feel agitated, sad, trapped in darkness, and spiritually desolate.

Choose •

Today, I choose the way of loving consolation.

I slowly and prayerfully read the scripture text below:

> If then there is any encouragement in Christ, any consolation from love, any sharing in the Spirit, any compassion and sympathy, make my joy complete: be of the same mind, having the same love, being in full accord

and of one mind. Do nothing from selfish ambition or conceit, but in humility regard others as better than yourselves. Let each of you look not to your own interests, but to the interests of others. Let the same mind be in you that was in Christ Jesus. (Phil 2:1–4)

I choose, in three thoughtful steps, the direction I wish to take:

I choose to follow the way of revival, led by the good spirit, toward love.

I reject desolation, being led into darkness and disturbed by the bad spirit.

I turn and walk in the contrary direction, from being desolate to being consoled and revived.

Rest •
I rest in the reviving Spirit.

I imagine the Spirit addresses me, saying, "Trust God as Jesus did, having the same mind and the same love, and consolation will soon be yours."

So, I rest now in this consoling Spirit, feeling myself coming back to life with compassion, sympathy, and love growing in my mind and heart. I feel revived.

If I belong to a group seeking revival, we rest in this Spirit together.

Reach Out •
I reach out to those of like mind and heart.

I conclude in thanks, considering two questions. First, if possible, how might I reconnect with the one who consoled me? Second, to whom and how do I pass on this exercise? Who urgently needs spiritual revival now?

Exercise 15: **Understanding**

Touch •

I touch the heart of wisdom.

I hold a symbol of understanding and wisdom. Tribal markings on an aboriginal face map both identity and belief. I consider the different faces of wisdom that have marked my life journey: insight, good judgment, clear thinking, foresight, self-knowledge, and even spiritual discernment.

I recall a story of receiving spiritual wisdom when I needed it. If praying alone, I hold that memory. If I am praying in a group, I share it with them, listening in turn to their stories, feeling touched by the Spirit of Wisdom.

Desire •

I desire understanding.

I slowly and prayerfully read the scripture text below:

> Who is wise and understanding among you? Show by your good life that your works are done with gentleness born of wisdom. But if you have bitter envy and selfish ambition in your hearts, do not be boastful and false to the truth. Such wisdom does not come down from above, but is earthly, unspiritual, devilish. For where there is envy and selfish ambition, there will also be disorder and wickedness of every kind. But the wisdom from above is first pure, then peaceable, gentle, willing to yield, full of mercy and good fruits, without a trace of partiality or hypocrisy. And a harvest of righteousness is sown in peace for those who make peace. (Jas 3:13–18)

I name all the areas of my life and relationships that I wish to fill with wisdom.

I ask the Spirit for the gift of wisdom and discernment when my situation is inherently confused, muddied by hidden agendas, or riven by external conflict.

Breathe •

I breathe in the Spirit of Understanding.

I imagine and feel the Spirit of Understanding breathing insight, good judgment, and self-knowledge into me.

I breathe them in deeply, wait, and then breathe them out into my relationships, where gently understanding the one before me is the greater good.

I repeat as desired—breathing, understanding, peaceful....

If I belong to a group seeking wisdom, we breathe this Spirit in and out together.

Reach Out •

I reach out to those of like mind and heart.

I conclude in thanks, considering two questions. First, if possible, can I reconnect with the one who guided me with wisdom? Second, to whom and how do I pass on this exercise? Who urgently needs spiritual wisdom now?

Exercise 16: **Respect**

Touch •
I touch the heart of respect.

I take off my shoes, placing them in front of me, a sign of my respect for the sacred ground of this prayer. As I do this, I enter the presence of the Spirit of Respect.

I recall a story of someone who has really respected me, faults and all. If praying alone, I hold that memory. If I am praying in a group, I share it with them, feeling touched by the Spirit of Respect.

Desire •
I desire respect.

I slowly and prayerfully read the scripture text below:

> Encourage one another and build up each other, as you are doing. We appeal to you, brothers and sisters, to respect those who labour among you, esteem them very highly in love because of their work. Be at peace among yourselves. We urge you, beloved, to reprove the idlers, encourage the faint hearted, help the weak, be patient with all of them. See that none of you repays evil for evil, but always seek to do good to one another and to all. Rejoice always, pray without ceasing, give thanks in all circumstances; for this is the will of God in Christ Jesus for you. Do not quench the Spirit. (1 Thess 5:11–22)

I name all the ways I need respect.

I ask the Spirit to for the gift of respect, from God and from the people in my daily life, especially when I am ill or suffering from a wound. I want to stop putting myself down.

Respect •

I breathe in the Spirit of Respect.

I imagine and feel the Spirit breathing the gift of respect and reverence into me.

I breathe them in deeply, and then breathe them out into my bruised but loving heart, into all displaced people and into places of care and refuge.

I repeat as desired—breathing, respecting, encouraging....

If I belong to a group seeking to be respectful, we breathe this Spirit together.

Reach Out •

I reach out to those of like mind and heart.

I conclude in thanks, considering two questions. First, if possible, can I reconnect with the one who gave me respect? Second, to whom and how do I pass on this exercise? Who needs healing respect now?

Health Care

Health care is usually done in a doctor's room or at home, but a field hospital on the frontlines or in a disaster area treats large numbers of people needing health care. God's field hospital has a health care service of surprising simplicity—the healing of gentleness, generosity, forgiveness, and kindness.

Exercise 17: Salve of Gentleness. Harshness, severity, or violence never heals. A different relationship is necessary for healing, especially with my own illness. The Spirit of Gentleness is a salve for every kind of healing. Exercise 17 is for those wishing to be gentler with themselves, their illness, and with others.

Exercise 18: Antibiotic of Generosity. The strange thing about suffering bad health with few resources is that acts of generosity can heal. The Spirit of Generosity will fight the infection of wounded self-centeredness. Exercise 18 is for those seeking the antibiotic of generosity.

Exercise 19: Splint of Forgiveness. A common result of deep wounds is a past hurt that is unforgiven. The unforgiven person, sickness or event is like a cancer eating away at health. The Spirit of Forgiveness mends that which is broken. Exercise 19 is for those who need the splint of forgiveness to mend the bones of a new self.

Exercise 20: Bandage of Kindness. Loving kindness is inherently healing for both the giver and receiver. A simple movement of the heart reaching out to help or affirm another is a bandage of comfort and protection. The Spirit of Kindness wraps a wound with tender love. Exercise 20 is for those desiring the bandage of kindness.

Symptoms to Increase Health

Exercise 17. I wish to be gentle. I need to be more tender in my relationships. Power or force will not bring the healing I need. Anger and denial are making things worse. I need to be gentle.

Exercise 18. I seek to be more generous. When I am generous, my eyes look to another's needs. If I listen to another's pain, my ears heal my own heart. I desire to be more generous.

Exercise 19. I need to forgive and to be forgiven. I have wounds that never seem to heal, and my alienation from those I love grows daily. For such wounds, I desire both to be forgiven and to forgive.

Exercise 20. I desire to be kind. When I was little, my mother put a bandage on my hurt, dried my tears, and all was well. Now I need my mother's heart to heal others. I desire to be kinder.

Exercise 17: **Salve of Gentleness**

Touch •

I touch the heart of gentleness.

I take a flower petal and carefully examine it—the color, fragility, and wonder of it. Caressing it, I imagine it could be the wing of a butterfly or the cheek of a baby. Gently stroking the petal, I feel the Spirit of Gentleness quietly joining me.

I remember a small story of someone who was very gentle with me when I was full of anger, fear, or grief. If praying alone, I hold that memory. If I am praying in a group, I share it with them, feeling touched by the Spirit of Gentleness.

Desire •

I desire to be gentle.

I slowly and prayerfully read the scripture text below:

> Let your gentleness be known to everyone. The Lord is near. Do not worry about anything, but in everything by prayer and supplication with thanksgiving let your requests be made known to God. And the peace of God, which surpasses all understanding, will guard your hearts and your minds in Christ Jesus. (Phil 4:5–9)

I name all the relationships and situations where I desire to be gentle.

I ask the Spirit for the gift of gentleness—for a guarding peace in my heart and mind.

Breathe •

I breathe in the Spirit of Gentleness.

Then I imagine and feel the Spirit breathing gentleness and the peace of God into me.

I breathe them in deeply, wait, and then breathe them out to be gentle with my own needs, and out into all those needing a gentle touch in upset lives.

I repeat as desired—breathing, gently soothing, quiet peace....

If I belong to a group seeking gentleness, we breathe this Spirit in and out together.

Reach Out •

I reach out to those of like mind and heart.

I conclude in thanks, considering two questions. First, if possible, how might I reconnect with the one who gentled me? Second, to whom and how do I pass on this exercise? Who urgently needs gentleness now?

Exercise 18: **Antibiotic of Generosity**

Touch •
I touch the heart of generosity.

I hold some bread or rice. I consider how either is life to so many, and how bread broken, or rice shared, is a symbol of generosity. I slowly break the bread in two, or divide the rice into two lots, feeling, touching, and becoming deeply aware of my sharing actions. I feel the Spirit of Generosity moving in my hands.

I recall a story of someone who was incredibly generous to me when I was in want and urgent need. If praying alone, I hold that memory. If I am praying in a group, I share it with them, feeling touched by the Spirit of Generosity.

Desire •
I desire to be generous.

I slowly and prayerfully read the scripture text below:

> The day was drawing to a close, and the twelve disciples came to Jesus and said, "Send the crowd away, so that they may go into the surrounding villages and countryside, to lodge and get provisions; for we are here in a deserted place." But Jesus said to them, "You give them something to eat." They said, "We have no more than five loaves and two fish—unless we are to go and buy food for all these people." For there were about five thousand men. Taking the five loaves and the two fish, Jesus looked up to heaven, blessed and broke them, and gave them to the disciples to set before the crowd. All ate and were filled. What was left over was gathered up, twelve baskets of broken pieces. (Luke 9:12–17)

I name all the relationships and situations where I wish to be generous.

I ask the Spirit for the gift of overflowing generosity when I am called to be a generous, even if my resources are few, when the need of others is critical.

Breathe •

I breathe in the Spirit of Generosity.

I imagine and feel the Spirit breathing the gift of generosity into me.

I breathe it in deeply, wait, and then breathe it out into my relationships and service of others, and into those who hunger in body and spirit.

I repeat as desired—breathing, generous, feeding hungers....

If I belong to a group seeking to be generous, we breathe this Spirit together.

Reach Out •

I reach out to those of like mind and heart.

I conclude in thanks, considering two questions. First, if possible, how might I reconnect with the one who was so generous to me? Second, to whom and how do I pass on this exercise? Who urgently needs generosity now?

Exercise 19: **Splint of Forgiveness**

Touch •
I touch the heart of reconciliation.

I find an object that symbolizes forgiveness and reconciliation for me. Holding it, I consider how distressed I have been when snared in darkness and undeserving of forgiveness. Yet I was forgiven.

I recall a story of when my action had brought me shame and damaged important relationships, but I was forgiven. I remember how glad and peaceful I was afterward, and since. If praying alone, I hold that glad memory. If I am praying in a group, I share it with them, listening in turn to their stories, feeling touched by the Spirit of Forgiveness.

Desire •
I desire to forgive.

I slowly and prayerfully read the scripture text below:

> Answer me when I call, O God. You gave me room when I was in distress. Be gracious to me and hear my prayer. When you are disturbed, my people, do not sin; ponder it on your beds, and be silent. Offer right sacrifices and put your trust in the LORD. Let the light of your face shine on us, O LORD! You have put gladness in my heart more than when their grain and wine abound. I will both lie down and sleep in peace; for you alone, O LORD, make me lie down in safety. (Ps 4)

I name all the people I wish to forgive.

I humbly ask the Spirit for help to forgive those who have hurt me, and for the gladness and peace that comes with it.

Breathe •

I breathe in the Spirit of Forgiveness.

I imagine the Spirit of Forgiveness addressing me by name, saying, “The Light of my face shines on you, you are forgiven. Forgive others. Lie down in safety and sleep in peace.”

I imagine and feel the Spirit breathing forgiveness, gladness, and a fresh beginning into me.

I breathe them in deeply, wait, and then breathe them out through my sorrow, broken relationships, and self-condemnation.

I repeat as desired—breathing, forgiving, glad....

If I belong to a group seeking to forgive, we breathe this Spirit in and out together.

Reach Out •

I reach out to those of like mind and heart.

I conclude in thanks, considering two questions. First, if possible, how might I reconnect with the one who forgave me? Second, to whom and how do I pass on this exercise? Who urgently needs to forgive?

Exercise 20: **Bandage of Kindness**

Touch •

I touch the heart of kindness.

I hold a small cloth, handkerchief, or paper tissue—a symbol of kindness, reminding me of times when my tears were gently wiped away, a bloody scrape of flesh was softly cleaned, or the sweat of my illness dabbed away.

I recall a story of someone who was kind to me when I was hurt or caught in desperate times. If praying alone, I hold that memory. If I am praying in a group, I share it with them, listening to their stories, touched by the Spirit of Kindness.

Desire •

I desire to be kind.

I slowly and prayerfully read the scripture text below:

> Stretch out your hand to the poor, so that your blessing may be complete. Give graciously to all the living; do not withhold kindness even from the dead. Do not avoid those who weep but mourn with those who mourn. Do not hesitate to visit the sick, because for such deeds you will be loved. (Sir 7:32–35)

I name all the relationships and places that I desire to bandage with kindness. Bandages soothe pain, and protect, support, and keep wounds clean.

I ask the Spirit for the gift of loving kindness, to give and receive, especially when faced with wounds that need cleaning, or circumstances that threaten thoughtfulness.

Breathe •

I breathe in the Spirit of Kindness.

I imagine and feel the Spirit breathing goodness and loving kindness into me.

I breathe them in deeply, wait, and then breathe them out into my daily relationships, actions and woundedness. Then I breathe into all those who suffer a harsh or desperate life.

I repeat as desired—breathing, kind, bandaging wounds…

If I belong to a group seeking kindness, we breathe this Spirit in and out together.

Reach Out •

I reach out to those of like mind and heart.

I conclude in thanks, considering two questions. First, if possible, how might I reconnect with the one who was so kind to me? Second, to whom and how do I pass on this exercise? Who urgently needs loving kindness now?

Mental-Health Care

Mental-health care in society is provided by counselors who guide, teach, and support. In God's field hospital, the Spirit is the Counselor, Comforter, Guide, Teacher, and Speaker of Truth. These are all ancient names of the Spirit. Loving care, compassion, hope, and peace are the first gifts of the healing Spirit.

Exercise 21: Precious Care. Holding a newly born baby, feeling the warm hug of forgiveness or an old burden lifted, enjoying a garden, being loved, being released from inner demons—all these are precious. So am I. The Spirit of True Whispers will tell me this all day long. Exercise 21 is for those who have forgotten how precious they are.

Exercise 22: Self-Compassion. It is a paradox that when we have the least emotional resources, we often become very hard on ourselves. The first step in mental-health care is to love and accept oneself. The Spirit of Self-Compassion helps this process of care. Exercise 22 is for those who need to treat themselves better.

Exercise 23: Awakening Hope. Caught in the struggles of mental health, it can be easy to lose hope. The Spirit of God's field hospital is the Spirit who lives within us, the Spirit of assistance when we are overwhelmed by trials, the Spirit of life after a difficult birth. It is a Spirit of Sparkling Eyes. Exercise 23 is for those who need to hope again.

*Exercise 24: Serenity.** There is nothing more healing than laying back, letting go and resting peacefully in the arms, or heart, of someone who cares about you. In God's field hospital, the Spirit of Serenity will come to you. Exercise 24 is for those desiring inner peace in God.

Symptoms of Mental Health

Exercise 21. I feel unloved and worthless. I feel unwanted and unappreciated. Even those close to me seem to take me for granted, especially when I am ill. I desire nurturing, precious care.

Exercise 22. I am so hard on myself. Why do I treat myself in ways I would never treat another? How can I love myself, just as I am, even when ill? I want to be compassionate to myself.

Exercise 23. I need to hope again. When a small hole appears in one's plans, hope trickles out like water. As the hole grows, my old hopes are gone. I need a new and bigger hope.

Exercise 24. I am fractured and stressed. I am in turmoil, my emotions in disarray, and my mind runs in endless circles. The clamor of my ill health deafens me. I want to rest in God. I desire serenity.

Exercise 21: **Precious Care**

Touch •
I touch the heart of precious love.

I hold something precious to me. I choose not something rich in commercial value but something precious in my experience and life, perhaps something freely given or freely received.

I recall a story of being held as precious, a moment of precious care when I really needed it. If praying alone, I hold that memory. If I am praying in a group, I share it with them, listening in turn to their stories, feeling touched by the Spirit of Precious Care.

Desire •
I desire precious care.

I slowly and prayerfully read the scripture texts below:

> I tell you, my friends, are not five sparrows sold for two pennies? Yet not one of them is forgotten in God's sight. But even the hairs of your head are all counted. Do not be afraid; you are of more value than many sparrows. (Luke 12:4–6)

> How precious is your steadfast love, O God! All people may take refuge in the shadow of your wings. They feast on the abundance of your house, and you give them drink from the river of your delights. For with you is the fountain of life; in your light we see light. (Ps 36)

I name my needs—body, mind, and spirit—for steadfast, precious love.

Then, I ask the Spirit for a pastoral carer, to nurture, feed, and accompany me in my vulnerability and need, on my journey back to health and wellness.

Breathe •

I breathe in the Spirit of Loving Whispers.

I imagine the Spirit whispering to me, intimately, saying, "You are precious in my sight."

I imagine and feel the Spirit of pastoral care breathing empathy and healing into me. I breathe them in deeply, pause, and then breathe them out into my physical and mental health, to nurture and sustain me, especially when my strength fails in times of misery.

I repeat as desired—breathing, nourished, cared for....

If I belong to a group seeking care, we breathe this Spirit in and out together.

Reach Out •

I reach out to those of like mind and heart.

I conclude in thanks, considering two questions. First, if possible, how might I reconnect with the person who cared for me? Second, to whom and how do I pass on this exercise? Who needs precious pastoral care now?

Exercise 22: **Self-Compassion**

Touch •
I touch the heart of self-compassion.

I am created in the image of God. And the creative Spirit loves all that is created. So, I take a hand mirror and see in it both the wonderful image of God, and the equally wonderful image of myself. Contemplating my reflection, I consider self-acceptance.

I recall a story of radical acceptance by a person at a time or event when I thought so very little of myself. I recall the slow, warm flush of a new and deeper self-acceptance. If praying alone, I hold that transforming memory. If I am praying in a group, I share it with them, listening in turn to their stories, feeling touched by the Spirit of self-acceptance.

Desire •
I desire self-compassion.

I slowly and prayerfully read the scripture text below:

> Lord, you love all things that exist, and detest none of the things that you have made, for you would not have made anything if you had hated it. How would anything have endured if you had not willed it? Or how would anything not called forth by you have been preserved? You spare all things, for they are yours, O Lord, you who love the living. For your immortal spirit is in all things. (Wis 11:24—12:1)

I name all the things in myself that I wish a greater self-acceptance of....

I ask the Spirit for the healing of a gentle self-acceptance, a light touch with myself, a smile in the mirror to warm my heart.

Breathe •
I breathe in the Spirit of Self-Compassion.

I imagine the Spirit of Self-Compassion addresses me by name, saying, "I love you for I created you. My immortal spirit is in you. See yourself as I see you—utterly beautiful."

I breathe in deeply this gentle, loving acceptance, wait, and then breathe it out into my self-image and all those needing a transforming self-acceptance.

I repeat as desired—breathing, accepting, loved....

If I belong to a group seeking self-compassion, we breathe in this Spirit together.

Reach Out •
I reach out to those of like mind and heart.

I conclude in thanks, considering two questions. First, if possible, how might I reconnect with the one who helped me to accept myself? Second, to whom and how do I pass on this exercise? Who needs greater self-acceptance now?

Exercise 23: **Awakening Hope**

Touch •

I touch the heart of hope.

I blindfold myself. Unafraid, I feel the dark. I sense how I would need to trust the hand of a helper to make my way forward in this darkness. Symbolically, I wait in the dark in this prayer, as one full of hope, ready for the helping hand of the hopeful Spirit.

I recall a story of someone who gave me hope in dark times. If praying alone, I hold that memory. If I am praying in a group, I share it with them, listening in turn to their stories, feeling touched by the Spirit of Hope.

Desire •

I desire new hope.

I slowly and prayerfully read the scripture text below:

> Those who fear the Lord will not be timid, or play the coward, for he is their hope. The eyes of the Lord are on those who love him, a mighty shield and strong support, a shelter from scorching wind and a shade from noonday sun, a guard against stumbling and a help against falling. He lifts up the soul and makes the eyes sparkle; he gives health and life and blessing. (Sir 34:16–20)

I name all the relationships and situations where I desire hope.

I ask the hopeful Spirit for a patient and sure hope when I most need it—even in the dark, frightening, hopeless situations, when I feel overwhelmed. I beg the Spirit to bring back the sparkle in my eyes.

Breathe •

I breathe in the Spirit of Awakening Hope.

I imagine and feel the Spirit breathing the gift of hope into me.

I breathe it in deeply, wait, and then breathe it out to renew my life, to reseed my relationships with new growth, and to banish seemingly endless disappointment.

I repeat as desired—breathing, hopeful, growing toward the light...

If I belong to a group seeking hope, we breathe this Spirit in and out together.

Reach Out •

I reach out to those of like mind and heart.

I conclude in thanks, considering two questions. First, if possible, how do I reconnect with the one who made me feel so hopeful? Second, to whom and how do I pass on this exercise? Who really needs hope now?

Exercise 24: **Serenity***

Touch •
I touch the heart of quiet peace.

I find and hold an object that symbolizes tranquility, a restful peace, for me.

I recall a story of receiving serenity with the help of a friend when I needed it. If praying alone, I hold that memory. If I am praying in a group, I share it with them, listening in turn to their stories, feeling touched by the Spirit of Serenity.

Desire •
I desire serenity.

I consider three things, taking a few minutes to explore each of them. I ask myself:

Where do I rest in serenity with God?

Where am I agitated and cut off from God's care?

What, for me, is the contrary or opposite of serenity?

I ask for the Spirit for Serenity in the arms of my God whenever afflicted.

Choose •
I choose the way of serenity.

I slowly and prayerfully read the scripture text below:

> Return, O my soul, to your rest, for the LORD has dealt bountifully with you. For you have delivered my soul from death, my eyes from tears, my feet from stumbling I walk before the LORD in the land of the living. I kept my faith, even when I said, "I am greatly afflicted." (Ps 116)

I choose, in three thoughtful steps, the direction I wish to take:

I choose the way of serenity, led by the good spirit into God's arms.

I reject the restless way where I am beaten down by afflictions and diminished by the bad spirit.

I walk in the contrary direction, from agitation to calm and to serenity in God.

Rest •

I open myself to the Spirit of Serenity.

I imagine that the Spirit addresses me by name, saying, "Rest peacefully in me, be content, you are now safe."

So, I rest, now, and reflect through the whole day in the Spirit's quiet, peace, and assurance. I feel a joyous harmony singing in my life, both present and future.

If I belong to a group seeking quiet peace, we rest in this Spirit together.

Reach Out •

I reach out to those of like mind and heart.

I conclude in thanks, considering two questions. First, if possible, how might I reconnect with the one who led me into serenity? Second, to whom and how do I pass on this exercise? Who needs tranquility in God now?

III

Intensive Care

Critical Care

God's field hospital will accept anyone from any background without questions, even if that person has acted with injustice, is driven by inner demons, or lives without hope or faith. God welcomes such people. God's critical care is about freedom, intimacy, justice, and empowerment for new life.

Exercise 25: Freedom from Demons. There are demons within us that can drive us away from freedom, thoughts, and desires that chain and immobilize us, eventually in addictive habits. Thorn, shackle, and fear cripple our heart. The Spirit of Freedom unbinds us. Exercise 25 is for those who desire freedom from destructive spirits.

*Exercise 26: Intimacy with God.** The healing God is hands-on, personal in affections and actions. With such healing comes the greater gift of intimacy. In fact, it is this intimate relationship with God, unique to you, that heals the most. The Spirit of Intimacy is close in critical care. Exercise 26 is for those with a distant or absent God.

Exercise 27: Healing Justice. Healing in body or mind is a great but of less worth if the one suffering is in a situation of great injustice. Being hungry or naked, bruised or chained, and without any basic rights, creates deep wounds. The Spirit of Justice is critical to a healing humanity. Exercise 27 is for healing justice.

Exercise 28: Empowerment. Without power over one's life, with heavy oppression, healing must run the gauntlet of hopelessness and regression. Personal and communal empowerment energizes and helps the wounded and ill to break into a better life. The Spirit of Power awaits. Exercise 28 is for the powerless.

Symptoms that Are Critical

Exercise 25. I am oppressed and afraid. I am driven by desires, habits, and actions that cripple me. My inner demons are noisy and demanding. I want to be in my right mind, at peace. I desire freedom.

Exercise 26. I am searching for God. I have never been close to God. God seems so far away and absent from real life. What did I care? But now I need a friend. I desire intimacy with a personal God.

Exercise 27. I am unjustly treated. My basic rights of word and action, of food, shelter, and dignity are at stake. My humanity is counted less than wealth, power, or position. I desire justice.

Exercise 28. I am disempowered. I am faint with endless striving for a say about my life. My voice is unheard, my wants ignored, and my feet are weary. I desire empowerment.

Exercise 25: **Freedom from Demons**

Touch •
I touch the heart of exorcism.

I hold a thorn, a symbol of an inner "demon." Whether my demon is the "enemy of my human nature," as St. Ignatius would suggest, a dark thorn in my heart, or the result of my choices, there are times when I may feel desperate, tormented, and even unrestrained, hurting myself or others, living a life among the tombs of my dead dreams.

I recall a story of being freed of my fears and inner demons. I recall the healer who returned me to my right mind, to peace. If praying alone, I hold that memory. If I am praying in a group, I share it with them, listening in turn to their stories, feeling touched by the Spirit of Freedom.

Desire •
I desire freedom from demons.

I slowly and prayerfully read the scripture text below:

> Jesus commanded the unclean spirit to come out of the man. (For many times it had seized him; he was kept under guard and bound with chains and shackles, but he would break the bonds and be driven by the demon into the wilds.) The demons came out of the man and entered the swine, and the herd rushed down the steep bank into the lake and was drowned.
>
> The people came out to see what had happened, and when they came to Jesus, they found the man from whom the demons had gone sitting at the feet of Jesus, clothed and in his right mind. (Luke 8:29, 33–35)

I name all the tormenting demons from which I wish to be freed.

I ask the Spirit to be free of destructive spirits, of thorn, shackle, and fear.

Breathe •

I breathe in the Spirit of Freedom.

I imagine the Spirit addressing me by name, saying to my demons, "Be gone," and to my fears, "Be at peace. I have broken your chains and freed you from your pain."

I imagine and feel the Spirit breathing healing, quiet, and humanity into me. I breathe them in deeply, wait, and then breathe out my demons, fears, and destructive behaviors.

I repeat as desired—breathing, healing, peaceful in right mind....

If I belong to a group seeking freedom from shackles, we breathe this Spirit together.

Reach Out •

I reach out to those of like mind and heart.

I conclude in thanks, considering two questions. First, if possible, how might I reconnect with the person who freed me of destructive spirits? Second, to whom and how do I pass on this exercise? Who needs to be free of the demons assaulting them?

Exercise 26: **Intimacy with God***

Touch •

I touch the heart of intimacy with God.

I find and hold an object that symbolizes divine intimacy for me—a relationship as close as a parent and child might be, or two lovers recently aware of each other. I imagine the Spirit of Intimacy lifting me up close, even cheek to cheek.

I recall a story of someone who showed me real intimacy.

If praying alone, I hold that memory. If I am praying in a group, I share it with them, feeling touched by the Spirit of Intimacy.

Desire •

I desire intimacy with God.

I consider three things, taking a few minutes to explore each of them. I ask myself:

Where is intimacy with God present in my life?

Where is intimacy with God absent in my life?

What, for me, is the contrary or opposite of intimacy with God?

I ask the Spirit for the gift of intimacy, especially when I am feeling unloved, alone, or drawn to actions that will cut me off from God's loving, personal presence.

Choose •

Today, I choose the way of intimacy.

I slowly and prayerfully read the scripture text below:

It was I [the Lord], who taught Ephraim to walk, I took them up in my arms; but they did not know that I healed them. I led them with cords of human kindness, with bands of love. I was to them like those who lift infants to their cheeks. I bent down to them and fed them. (Hos 11:3–4)

I choose, in three thoughtful steps, the direction I wish to take:

I choose to follow the way of intimacy, relishing the enfolding arms of God.

I reject the way of alienation, of being separated from God and tricked by a bad spirit.

I turn and walk in the contrary direction, from separation, to intimacy, to deep peace.

Rest •

I rest in the Spirit of Intimacy.

I imagine the Intimate Spirit who addresses me by name saying, "I would love it if we could each give and receive from one another our affection and our love."

I rest briefly—now and reflectively throughout the whole day—in the intimate Spirit.

I am lifted, healed, fed, and loved.

If I belong to a group seeking intimacy with God, we rest in this Spirit together.

Reach Out •

I reach out to those of like mind and heart.

I conclude in thanks, considering two questions. First, if possible, how might I reconnect with the one who was so intimate with me? Second, to whom and how do I pass on this exercise? Who urgently needs intimacy with the Spirit now?

Exercise 27: **Healing Justice**

Touch •
I touch the heart of justice.

I take up a small, straight stick and balance it on my finger, like the balance beam on a set of scales, the universal symbol of justice. Let finding that balance point with my stick bring me into a felt relationship with the Spirit of Justice. I imagine it so.

I recall a story of receiving justice or being just. If praying alone, I hold that memory. If I am praying in a group, I share it with them, listening in turn to their stories, feeling the Spirit of Justice take root in me.

Desire •
I desire healing justice.

I slowly and prayerfully read the scripture text below:

> The crowds followed Jesus, and he cured all of them. This was to fulfil what had been spoken through the prophet Isaiah: "Here is my servant, whom I have chosen, my beloved, with whom my soul is well pleased. I will put my Spirit upon him, and he will proclaim justice to the Gentiles. He will not wrangle or cry aloud, nor will anyone hear his voice in the streets. He will not break a bruised reed or quench a smouldering wick until he brings justice to victory." (Matt 12:15–41)

I name the justice that I seek and all the injustices that I feel and see around me.

I ask the Spirit for justice and a faith to support it.

Breathe •

I breathe in the Spirit of Justice.

I imagine the Spirit addressing me by name, saying, "You are my family. You will not be crushed by life events. Believe me, I will come to you."

I imagine and feel the Spirit breathing justice and faith into my life. I breathe them in deeply, wait, and then breathe it out into all the unjust structures, laws and relationships that surround me, into my own unjust heart.

I repeat as desired—breathing, just, fair....

If I belong to a group seeking justice, we breathe this Spirit together.

Reach Out •

I reach out to those of like mind and heart.

I conclude in thanks, considering two questions. First, if possible, how might I reconnect with the person who gave me justice? Second, to whom and how do I pass on this exercise? Who urgently needs justice now?

Exercise 28: **Empowerment**

Touch •

I touch the heart of empowerment.

I hold a feather, light, strong, and beautiful. I consider how being empowered lifts me up on wings of strength and self-determination, how it infuses me with the Spirit of Power and Love.

I recall a story of being empowered when I was down and powerless. If praying alone, I hold that memory. If I am praying in a group, I share it with them, listening in turn to their stories, feeling touched by the Spirit of Power.

Desire •

I desire to be empowered.

I slowly and prayerfully read the scripture text below:

> Have you not known? Have you not heard? The LORD is the everlasting God, the Creator of the ends of the earth. He does not faint or grow weary; his understanding is unsearchable. He gives power to the faint and strengthens the powerless. Even youths will faint and be weary, and the young will fall exhausted; but those who wait for the LORD shall renew their strength, they shall mount up with wings like eagles, they shall run and not be weary, they shall walk and not faint. (Ps 40)

I name all the people I want to empower, including myself.

I ask the Spirit for the power of choice and self-determination, for wings to lift me up.

Desire •
I breathe in the Spirit of Power.

I imagine and feel the Spirit of Power breathing strength, resilience, and the fullness of God's love into me.

I breathe them in deeply, wait, and then breathe them out to flow through my need and the need of all those who desire empowerment and support.

I repeat as desired—breathing, empowered, lifted....

If I belong to a group seeking empowerment, we breathe this Spirit together.

Reach Out •
I reach out to those of like mind and heart.

I conclude in thanks, considering two questions. First, if possible, how might I reconnect with the one who empowered me? Second, to whom and how do I pass on this exercise? Who needs empowerment and to be lifted?

Surgical Care

Surgical care is the treatment for acute injury or disease by operations. A scalpel incises the skin and opens the body to reveal and heal the interior wound. God's healing cleaves heart, bone and desire. It cuts through darkness and disorder. It is a sharp scalpel that seeks, finds, opens and releases new life.

*Exercise 29: Seeking Clarity.** With life-threatening illness comes great need and desperation. There are swirling emotions, dark memories, and debilitating confusion. Even with surgery, we sit in darkness. The Spirit of Clarity is a blade of Light. Exercise 29 excises the cancer of confusion with the blade of spiritual clarity.

*Exercise 30: Finding Courage.** Crippling fear is like an infection that spreads into every part of the body. Big fears multiply into small fears that poison everything. The Spirit of Courage dispels such toxic fear. A form of heart surgery, spiritual courage strengthens body, desire, and spirit. Exercise 30 is for those seeking spiritual courage.

*Exercise 31: Opening Light.** The operating room is dominated by the huge light above the operating table. Surgeons wear additional lights to see every body part clearly. So too, God's Light pierces the interior darkness of one's life, missing nothing. The Spirit of Light makes its home in us. Exercise 31 banishes the dark.

*Exercise 32: Releasing Energy.** The feeling and experience of depletion when sick makes living with disease so much harder. We may feel utterly emptied. The Spirit of Energy gives us the power to move again, lifting, singing, sparking, dancing, alive in us, even in ill health. Exercise 32 is for the gift of God's spiritual energy.

Symptoms for Surgery

Exercise 29. I need clarity of mind. My need for healing is evident. I need surgery. What is not clear is the confusion I feel about the way back to health and peace. I desire a clarity that heals.

Exercise 30. I need courage of heart. I am afraid of my healing, scared to lose control over my body, anxious about the changes I need, and panicking about tomorrow. I desire enduring courage.

Exercise 31. I need light for my soul. I am blind in my sickness. My future is out of focus. Darkness swirls around me and settles in me. I so need enlightenment. I desire to be filled with God's Light.

Exercise 32. I need spiritual energy. I am exhausted in body and spirit. I do not have the energy to change anything. My wounds, my illness exhaust me. I desire the strength of spiritual energy.

Exercise 29: **Seeking Clarity***

Touch •
I touch the heart of clarity.

I find and hold an object that symbolizes clarity for me. I consider how precious clarity is when choices need to be made or a path taken. I ponder what God desires for me in these situations. I need the Spirit's gift of clarity to discern my way forward.

I recall a story of receiving the help of spiritual clarity when I was tangled up and confused. If praying alone, I hold that memory. If I am praying in a group, I share it with them, listening in turn to their stories, feeling touched by the Spirit of Clarity.

Desire •
I desire spiritual clarity.

I consider three things, taking a few minutes to explore each of them. I ask myself:

Where is clarity present in my life?

Where is clarity absent in my life?

What, for me, is the contrary or opposite of clarity?

I ask the Spirit for the gift of spiritual clarity to discern the best way forward.

Choose •
I seek the way of spiritual clarity.

I slowly and prayerfully read the scripture text below:

> The way of the wicked is like deep darkness; they do not know what they stumble over. My child, be attentive to my words. Do not let them escape from your sight; keep them within your heart. For they are life to those who find them, and healing to all their flesh. Keep your

heart with all vigilance, for from it flow the springs of life. Let your eyes look directly forward, and your gaze be straight before you. Keep straight the path of your feet, and all your ways will be sure. Do not swerve; turn your foot away from evil. (Prov 4:19–27)

I choose, in three thoughtful steps, the direction I wish to take:

I choose to follow the clear, focused way of the good spirit, toward God's love.

I reject the obscure way, the confusion, and spurious objections of the bad spirit.

I turn and walk in the opposite direction from confusion to clarity and wise action.

Rest •
I rest in the Spirit of Clarity.

I imagine the Spirit of Clarity addresses me by name, saying, "I will help you to discern the best and clearest way forward."

So, I rest—now and reflectively throughout the whole day—in the clarity of the Spirit. I feel focused and clearer about the movements of the good spirit.

If I belong to a group seeking clarity, we rest in this Spirit together.

Reach Out •
I reach out to those of like mind and heart.

I conclude in thanks, considering two questions. First, if possible, how might I reconnect with the person who gave me clarity? Second, to whom and how do I pass on this exercise? Who urgently needs spiritual clarity now?

Exercise 30: **Finding Courage***

Touch •

I touch the heart of spiritual courage.

I hold an object that symbolizes spiritual courage for me.

I recall a story of receiving heartfelt courage when I needed it. If praying alone, I hold that memory. If I am praying in a group, I share it with them, listening in turn to their stories, feeling touched by the Spirit of Courage.

Desire •

I desire spiritual courage.

I consider three things, taking a few minutes exploring each. I ask myself:

> Where is spiritual courage present in my life?
>
> Where is spiritual courage absent in my life?
>
> What, for me, is the contrary or opposite of spiritual courage?

I ask the Spirit of Courage to give me the gift of courage, especially when I begin to lose heart in the face of great needs, loss of certainty, or critical health care.

Choose •

Today, I choose the way of courage.

I slowly and prayerfully read the scripture text below:

> A woman who had been suffering from haemorrhages for twelve years spent all she had on physicians, but no one could cure her. She came up behind Jesus and touched the fringe of his clothes, and immediately her haemorrhage stopped. Jesus asked, "Who touched me?" When the woman saw that she could not remain hid-

den, she came trembling; and falling down before him, she declared in the presence of all the people why she had touched him, and how she had been immediately healed. He said to her, "Daughter, your faith has made you well; go in peace." (Luke 8:42–48)

I choose, in three thoughtful steps, the direction I wish to take:

I choose to follow the way of courage led by the good spirit toward God's love.

I reject the way of fear and timidity, of being harassed by the bad spirit.

I turn and walk in the opposite direction from fear to courage and peace.

Rest •

I rest in the Spirit of Courage.

I imagine the Spirit addresses me, saying, "Be strong, take courage, I am with you."

So, I rest—now and reflectively throughout the whole day—in the Spirit's encouragement and promise. I feel braver and supported by the Spirit.

If I belong to a group seeking courage, we rest in this Spirit in and out together.

Reach Out •

I reach out to those of like mind and heart.

I conclude in thanks, considering two things. First, if possible, how might I reconnect with the one who encouraged me? Second, to whom and how do I pass on this exercise? Who urgently needs spiritual courage now?

Exercise 31: **Opening Light***

Touch •
I touch the heart of Light.

I find and hold an object that symbolizes the Light of God for me. I consider how this Light can be both enlightening my heart within me and shining in darkness from without of me.

I recall a story of receiving light when I was stumbling and afraid in the dark.

If praying alone, I hold that memory. If I am praying in a group, I share it with them, listening in turn to their stories, feeling touched by the Spirit of Light.

Desire •
I desire spiritual light.

I consider three things, taking a few minutes exploring each. I ask myself:

Where is the light of God present in my life?

Where is light of God absent in my life?

What, for me, is the contrary or opposite of the Light of God?

I ask the Spirit for the gift of Light, to see what is good, right, and true, to expose the works of darkness from within and without of me.

Choose •
Today, I choose the way of light.

I slowly and prayerfully read the scripture text below:

Once you were darkness, but now in the Lord you are light. Live as children of light, for the fruit of the light is found in all that is good and right and true. Try to find out what is pleasing to the Lord. Take no part in the unfruitful works of darkness, but instead expose them. Everything exposed by the light becomes visible, for everything that becomes visible is light. Therefore, it is said, "Sleeper, awake! Rise from the dead, and Christ will shine on you." (Eph 5:8–14)

I choose, in three thoughtful steps, the direction I wish to take:

I choose to follow the way of light, of the good spirit, into Christ's shining Light.

I reject the way of darkness, of being blinded by a bad spirit.

I turn and walk in the contrary direction, from dark to light, to shining bright.

Rest •

I rest in the Spirit of Light.

I imagine the Spirit of Light addressing me by name, saying, "Awaken. Rise from the dead. You are a child of Light."

So, I rest—now and reflectively throughout the whole day—in the good, right, and true Light of the Spirit. I feel my heart brighten and break free of binding darkness.

If I belong to a group seeking Light, we rest in this Spirit together.

Reach Out •

I reach out to those of like mind and heart.

I conclude in thanks, considering two questions. First, if possible, how might I reconnect with the person who gave me light? Second, to whom and how do I pass on this exercise? Who urgently needs Light now?

Exercise 32: **Releasing Energy***

Touch •

I touch the Spirit of Energy.

I hold an object that symbolizes spiritual energy for me. I consider all the ways this energy of the Spirit works within me—quick as a flash, slow like a sunrise, arcing across differences, weaving life threads, lifting, recreating, filling, and singing. How else does the Spirit work within me?

I recall a story of being energized by the Spirit, directly or through another, when I was listless and apathetic in my spiritual life. If praying alone, I hold that memory. If I am praying in a group, I share it with them, listening in turn to their stories, feeling touched by the flame of the Spirit.

Desire •

I desire spiritual energy.

I consider three things, taking a few minutes to explore each of them. I consider:

Where is spiritual energy present in my life?

Where is spiritual energy absent in my life?

What, for me, is the contrary or opposite of spiritual energy?

I ask the Spirit for the gift of spiritual energy.

Choose •

Today, I choose the way of spiritual energy.

I slowly and prayerfully read the scripture text below:

It was God's purpose to reveal to his people how rich is the glory of this mystery among the gentiles; it is Christ among you, your hope of glory: this is the Christ we are proclaiming, admonishing and instructing everyone in all wisdom, to make everyone perfect in Christ. And it is for this reason that I labour, striving with his energy which works in me mightily. (Col 1:27–29)

I choose, in three thoughtful steps, the direction I wish to take:

I choose to work with God's energy and power.

I reject the way of spiritual tepidity, of paralysis and apathy, led by a bad spirit.

I turn and walk in the opposite direction from sloth to energy and action.

Rest •

I rest in the Spirit of Energy.

I imagine the Spirit addressing me by name, saying, "I will work mightily in you."

So, I rest—now and reflectively throughout the whole day—in the Spirit's boundless energy. I feel empowered and fully alive.

If I belong to a group seeking spiritual energy, we rest in this Spirit together.

Reach Out •

I reach out to those of like mind and heart.

I conclude in thanks, considering two questions. First, if possible, how might I reconnect with the person who energized me in the Spirit? Second, to whom and how do I pass on this exercise? Who urgently needs spiritual energy now?

Coronary Care

God's field hospital specializes in heart-to-heart healing. God knows what is inside every human heart and, knowing all, chooses to love each heart just as it is. God's field hospital welcomes the sore heart, the wounded heart, and the brokenhearted. God's sacred heart flows with blood and water, love and life.

Exercise 33: Humble Heart. Heart diseases, hard-hearted relationships, half-hearted love, and divided hearts are often found underneath other sickness and wounds. But a clean heart, a loving heart, a pure heart, a heart of tears, these are humble remedies. For the Spirit of Humility heals wounds. Exercise 33 is for this humility.

Exercise 34: Rich Heart. When are we richest? A rich heart is not one full of things to live for, but one that gives out of its poverty—it no longer clings to itself. Paradoxically, the wounded become a healer. The Spirit of the Poor is generous. Exercise 34 offers the medicine of generosity.

Exercise 35: Laughing Heart. It is free, everyone has it and it can heal in any situation. It is the gift of laughter! God's field hospital, like all hospitals, is full of three things: pain, healing, and laughter, often happening in the last place you would expect. The Spirit of Laughter is a nurse. Exercise 35 is for those needing to laugh.

*Exercise 36: Passionate Heart.** When you are suffering or wounded, all the niceties about a relationship with God disappear. A raw need just to be held by God, to taste the fire of God's passionate care, and to speak the unspeakable need surge up. The Spirit of Passion is spark, flame, and ember. Exercise 36 is for passionate hearts.

Symptoms of the Heart

Exercise 33. I need humility. I am proud of myself, my work, and my possessions. But now, I am ill and in need of help. I realize my heart has been selfish. I desire a contrite, humble heart.

Exercise 34. I need to be generous. My illness has emptied my heart. I am desperate for good health, but I keep filling it with unnecessary, self-centered things. To heal, I need a generous heart.

Exercise 35. I need to laugh again. Laughter is spontaneous when it spills light into the darkness of my suffering. Leaping from the belly and heart, it heals me. I desire a laughing heart.

Exercise 36. I need to be loved with passion. I do not need to *know* God loves me. I am sick. I need to *feel* God's love—not a tepid love, but a wild embrace to hold me now. I desire God's passionate heart.

Exercise 33: **Humble Heart**

Touch •

I touch the heart of humility.

I ask a small child to draw the three most important things in life. Jesus knew that a child under twelve in his day had no status or prestige. A child's drawing of important things is likely to take a *humble* view, unconcerned about status, ego, or pride. As I hold it, I consider the last time I was genuinely humble, and before whom?

I recall a story of a person teaching me humility. If praying alone, I hold that memory. If I am praying in a group, I share it with them, listening in turn to their stories and feeling touched by the Spirit of Humility.

Desire •

I desire a humble heart.

I slowly and prayerfully read the scripture text below:

> The disciples came to Jesus and asked, "Who is the greatest in the kingdom of heaven?" He called a child, whom he put among them, and said, "Truly I tell you, unless you change and become like children, you will never enter the kingdom of heaven. Whoever becomes humble like this child is the greatest in the kingdom of heaven. Whoever welcomes one such child in my name welcomes me." (Matt 18:1–5)

I name all the things in myself and my relationships for which I seek humility.

I ask the Spirit for a humble heart, to learn from the "little ones" in society—young,old, charitable, poor, educated, or uneducated—who already know humility.

Breathe •

I breathe in the Spirit of Humility.

I imagine the Spirit addressing me by name, saying, "Blessed are the pure in heart: they shall see God."

So, I breathe the Spirit's honesty and regard for others in deeply, wait, and then breathe greater humility out into my relationships, and into those who are blinded and diminished by pride, ego, and self-satisfaction.

I repeat as desired—breathing, humble, earthed...

If I belong to a group seeking humility, we breathe this Spirit together.

Reach Out •

I reach out to those of like mind and heart.

I conclude in thanks, considering two questions. First, if possible, how might I reconnect with the one who helped me to be humble? Second, to whom and how do I pass on this exercise? Who urgently needs the healing of a humble heart?

Exercise 34: **Rich Heart**

Touch •

I touch the heart of poverty.

I hold the smallest coin in my currency. It has two sides, a symbol of the two faces of poverty. I consider the first side—actual poverty in all its forms—financial, disability, literacy, cultural, loss of rights, and spiritual poverty. Turning the coin, I consider the other side of poverty, the poor themselves, and the "riches" they have to offer me.

I recall a story of a person who taught me the rich heart of the poor. If praying alone, I hold that memory. If I am praying in a group, I share it with them, listening in turn to their stories, feeling touched by the Spirit of Poverty.

Desire •

I desire a rich heart.

I slowly and prayerfully read the scripture text below:

> Jesus watched the crowd putting money into the temple treasury. Many rich people put in large sums. A poor widow came and put in two small copper coins, which are worth a penny. Then he called his disciples and said to them, "Truly I tell you; this poor widow has put in more than all those who are contributing to the treasury. For all of them have contributed out of their abundance; but she out of her poverty has put in everything she had, all she had to live on." (Mark 12:41–44)

I name all the things I wish to give from both my riches and my poverty.

I ask the Spirit for a rich heart, like the poor, to offer those in need all that I have or can give.

Breathe •

I breathe the Spirit of the poor.

I imagine the Spirit addressing me by name, saying, "Blessed are the poor in spirit: the kingdom of Heaven is theirs."

Then I imagine the Spirit breathing generosity and faith into me. I breathe them in deeply, wait, and then breathe them out over my hands to release tight fists, and into my heart to learn from the poor.

I repeat as desired—breathing, rich and poor, generous/...

If I belong to a group seeking a rich heart, we breathe this Spirit together.

Reach Out •

I reach out to those of like mind and heart.

I conclude in thanks, considering two questions. First, if possible, how might I reconnect with the one who showed me the heart of the poor? Second, to whom and how do I pass on this exercise? Who may appreciate the healing of a richer heart?

Exercise 35: **Laughing Heart**

Touch •
I touch the heart of laughter.

I hold a smile, the symbol of laughter and joy. A contagious smile releases the muscles of my face and my heart. I remember the last thing that brought a smile to my face. Then I ponder the variety of laughter, from grin to chuckle to roar.

I recall a story of someone who makes me laugh, even in the darkest of places, when sadness or heavy responsibilities overwhelm me. If praying alone, I hold that memory. If I am praying in a group, I share it with them, listening in turn to their stories, feeling touched by the Spirit of Laughter.

Desire •
I desire a laughing heart.

I slowly and prayerfully read the scripture text below:

> They had come to hear Jesus and to be healed of their diseases; and those who were troubled with unclean spirits were cured. And all in the crowd were trying to touch him, for power came out from him and healed all of them. Then he looked up at his disciples and said: "Blessed are you who are poor, for yours is the kingdom of God. Blessed are you who weep now, for you will laugh." (Luke 6:18–21)

I name all the relationships, commitments, and places in my life where I wish laughter to be heard.

I ask the Spirit for the gift of laughter, a sense of humor, and a heart in balance. I consider how laughter heals, humanizes, and liberates—how close it is to wonder.

Breathe •
I breathe in the Spirit of Laughter.

I imagine and feel the Spirit of Laughter breathing release, joy, and delight into me.

I breathe them in deeply, wait, and then breathe them out through my sadness or tears.

I repeat as desired—breathing, smiling, happier....

If I belong to a group seeking the gift of laughter, we breathe this Spirit together.

Reach Out •
I reach out to those of like mind and heart.

I conclude in thanks, considering two questions. First, if possible, how might I reconnect with the one who made me laugh? Second, to whom and how do I pass on this exercise? Who would appreciate healing laughter now?

Exercise 36: **Passionate Heart***

Touch •
I touch the heart of passionate love.

I find and hold an object that symbolizes the passionate love. I consider how love will always seek and find the lover, for such love is as strong as death.

I recall a story of being shown, or experiencing, the passionate love of God.

If praying alone, I hold that memory. If I am praying in a group, I share it with them, listening in turn to their stories, feeling touched by the flame of the Spirit.

Desire •
I desire a passionate heart.

I consider three things, taking a few minutes exploring each. I ask myself:

Where is the love of God flaring in my life?

Where is the love of God absent in my life?

What, for me, is the contrary or opposite of the passionate love of God?

I ask the Spirit for the blazing love of my Creator and Lord, an intense love that sweeps all else away, so that I may love only what the Lord desires for me.

Choose •
Today, I choose the way of fire.

I slowly and prayerfully read the scripture text below:

> Set me as a seal upon your heart, as a seal upon your arm; for love is strong as death, passion fierce as the grave. Its flashes are flashes of fire, a raging flame....I

will seek him whom my soul loves....The sentinels found me, as they went about in the city. "Have you seen him whom my soul loves?" Scarcely had I passed them, when I found him whom my soul loves. I held him and would not let him go. (Song of Songs 8:6–7; 3:2–4)

I choose, in three thoughtful steps, the direction I wish to take:

I choose fire and passion in my love of God and love of others led by the good spirit.

I reject the way of a dark, joyless separation from God and a bleak heart led by a bad spirit.

I turn and walk in the opposite direction from gloom to fiery love and intimacy.

Rest •

I rest in the Spirit of Passion.

I imagine the Spirit addressing me by name, saying, "I will dance on the crown of your head, in a tongue of flame, to call you out of yourself and send you out to dispel the works of darkness."

So, I rest—now and reflectively throughout the whole day—feeling my heart catch alight in the wild and desiring love of the passionate Spirit.

If I belong to a group seeking God's passionate love, we rest in this Spirit together.

Reach Out •

I reach out to those of like mind and heart.

I conclude in thanks, considering two questions. First, if possible, how might I reconnect with the person who showed me the passionate love of God. Second, to whom and how do I pass on this exercise? Who urgently needs the healing of God's ardent love?

IV

Specialist Care

Respiratory Care

We breathe to live. So, the Spirit of God is called the Breath of God. God's breath breathes life back into us. If our breathing is blocked, we choke and die. Western and Eastern Christianity have long traditions of praying with breath. Breathing prayer offers transformation, relaxation, liberation, and great peace.

Exercise 37: Transforming Breath. People often say to someone who is ill, "I hope you get back to being your old self." Unfortunately, serious illness or near-death experiences change us. We will never be the same, but we can be something new. The Spirit of Transformation is powerful. Exercise 37 is for finding life after feeling dead.

Exercise 38: Relaxing Breath. It is said that with stress one needs "flight or fight" for resolution. But being wounded and ill, the sick can do neither. Stress flows through every thought, and anxieties spill into every action. Life is strangled. God's field hospital has the Spirit of Relaxation. Exercise 38 is for breathing freely again.

Exercise 39: Liberating Breath. God releases even strangers from the bondage of illness. God sets free those who are alone and wounded. They are especially welcome. The Spirit of Liberation makes its home in them. Exercise 39 is for those imprisoned by suffering.

Exercise 40: Peaceful Breath. Tranquility and peace are special gifts for those made wretched by illness. Job, an ancient believer, said, "I have the breath of God in my nostrils." This Spirit of Peace clears away the snot of worry and the blockages of depression. Exercise 40 is for inhaling the harmony of love and for breathing peacefully.

Symptoms of Blocked Breathing

Exercise 37. I need a life that is transforming. I feel like bones in a desert—my health and well-being leached out of me. I need fresh life, a resurrection from my debilitating sickness.

Exercise 38. I need some release from stress. I suffer from anxiety, sometimes even panic attacks. My illness, my wound, and my everyday vulnerability terrorizes me. I feel endlessly afraid. I just want to relax.

Exercise 39. I need liberation from my prison. I am in the prison of chronic illness, disease, and loss. I need someone to unlock my cell door, lift my burden, and break me out.

Exercise 40. I need cleansing peace. I seem to lurch from one crisis to another, and from one health problem to another. I desire God's cleansing peace washing through me. I seek peace of mind.

Exercise 37: **Transforming Breath**

Touch •
I touch the heart of transformation.

I hold a stone in one hand and a living thing in the other. I consider how God can transform a stony heart into a heart of flesh, something dead into something living.

I recall a story of being transformed back to life when I felt as lifeless as dry bones in a desert. If praying alone, I hold that memory. If I am praying in a group, I share it with them, listening in turn to their stories, feeling touched by the Spirit of Transformation.

Desire •
I desire a transforming breath.

I slowly and prayerfully read the scripture text below:

> The LORD set me down in the middle of a valley full of bones, saying, "I will cause breath to enter you, and you shall live. I will lay sinews on you, and cause flesh to come upon you, and cover you with skin, and put breath in you, and you shall live; and you shall know that I am the LORD." I prophesied as he commanded me, and the breath came into them, they lived, and stood on their feet, a vast multitude....Then he said to me, "Therefore prophesy, and say to them, Thus says the LORD GOD: I am going to open your graves, and bring you up from your graves, O my people." (Ezek 37:1–13)

I name all the parts of my life that I wish God to restore. I ask the Spirit for the grace to be utterly transformed.

Breathe •

I breathe in the Spirit of Transformation.

I imagine the Spirit of Transformation breathing new life into me, awakening all that I thought was dead in me, transforming me into someone with a new, courageous, and daring heart.

I breathe in the breath of the Spirit, pause, and then breathe out through my life, and into all those needing a new start in life amid death in any form and want.

I repeat as desired—breathing, enlivening, transforming....

If I belong to a group seeking transforming life, we breathe this Spirit together.

Reach Out •

I reach out to those of like mind and heart.

I conclude in thanks, considering two questions. First, if possible, how might reconnect with the one who brought me back to life? Second, to whom and how do I pass on this exercise? Who needs the breath of new life now?

Exercise 38: **Relaxing Breath**

Touch •
I touch the heart of relaxion.

I find something that symbolizes release from the bondage of stress. Holding it, I consider the various ways that stress shackles me and affects my relationships, and how freedom from such stress will restore my energy so that I can live my life more fully.

I recall a story of being released from stress when I was chained up and living in some form of emotional or physical bondage. If praying alone, I hold that memory. If I am praying in a group, I share it with them, listening in turn to their stories. Feeling touched by the Spirit of Relaxation, I begin to see myself flying free.

Desire •
I desire a relaxing breath.

I slowly and prayerfully read the scripture text below:

> My heart is in anguish within me, the terrors of death have fallen upon me. Fear and trembling come upon me, and horror overwhelms me. And I say, "O that I had wings like a dove! I would fly away and be at rest. I would hurry to find a shelter for myself from the raging wind and tempest." ...But I call upon God, and the LORD will save me. Cast your burden on the LORD, and he will sustain you. (Ps 55)

I name all the chains and burdens from which I wish to be free.

I ask the Spirit to free me from fear, trembling, terror, and being overwhelmed.

Breathe •

I breathe in the Spirit of Relaxation.

I imagine the Spirit of Relaxation addressing me by name, saying, "Your light will break forth like the dawn, and your healing will spring up quickly."

I breathe in this light and healing, wait, and then breathe it out into my stressors, into all that chains me up, and I see those chains break. I fly free, released, and whole.

I repeat as desired—breathing, releasing stress, relaxing....

If I belong to a group seeking spiritual energy, we breathe this Spirit together.

Reach Out •

I reach out to those of like mind and heart.

I conclude in thanks, considering two questions. First, if possible, how might I reconnect with the one who released me from the chains of stress? Second, to whom and how do I pass on this exercise? Who urgently needs to be freed from their bonds?

Exercise 39: **Liberating Breath**

Touch •
I touch the heart of freedom.

I hold a key, a symbol of freedom from imprisonment—physical, emotional, or spiritual. I consider how we are born with equal freedom—yet we live with unlawful detentions, tribal violence, abuse, and racism, even genocide. As I hold the key, I consider all the places and relationships where I am locked up.

I recall a small story of being freed by someone from a prison of body, mind, or spirit. If praying alone, I hold that memory. If I am praying in a group, I share it with them, listening in turn to their stories, feeling touched by the Spirit of Freedom.

Desire •
I desire a liberating breath.

I slowly and prayerfully read the scripture text below:

> Happy are those whose hope is in the Lord their God; who made heaven and earth, the sea, and all that is in them; who keeps faith forever; who executes justice for the oppressed; who gives food to the hungry. The LORD sets the prisoners free; the LORD opens the eyes of the blind. The LORD lifts up those who are bowed down; the LORD loves the righteous. The LORD watches over the strangers; he upholds the orphan and the widow. (Ps 146: 5–9)

Unlocking my heart, I name all the freedoms that I desire.

I ask the Spirit for liberation, both interior and exterior. I desire to turn the key in the door of my soul and discover the riches within. I desire to free my energies to serve.

Breathe •

I breathe in the Spirit of Liberation.

I imagine the Spirit addressing me by name, saying, "I will set you free from all that oppresses and imprisons you."

I imagine and feel the Spirit breathing light, freedom, and release into me.

I breathe them in deeply, wait, and then breathe them out to turn the key to my heart and open my full potential, to liberate me and all those who are imprisoned.

I repeat as desired—breathing, unlocking, free....

If I belong to a group seeking liberation, we breathe this Spirit together.

Reach Out •

I reach out to those of like mind and heart.

I conclude in thanks, considering two questions. First, if possible, how might I reconnect with the person who freed me from a prison? Second, to whom and how do I pass on this exercise? Who urgently needs liberation now?

Exercise 40: **Peaceful Breath**

Touch •

I touch the heart of peace.

I take a slow breath, in and out—a breath in to receive the Spirit of Peace, and a breath out to breathe out all the anxiety, agitation, fears, and burdens that I carry within me. This breath of body and spirit is life to me. I repeat, feeling peace settle in me.

I recall a small story of someone who gave me deep peace when I was afraid and distressed. If praying alone, I hold that memory. If I am praying in a group, I share it with them, listening in turn to their stories, feeling touched by the Spirit of Peace.

Desire •

I name parts of my life where I desire peace.

I slowly and prayerfully read the scripture text below:

> As God's chosen ones, holy and beloved, clothe yourselves with compassion, kindness, humility, meekness, and patience. Above all, clothe yourselves with love, which binds everything together in perfect harmony.... And let the peace of Christ rule in your hearts. (Col 3:12–16)

I ask the Spirit for peace, serenity, and harmony in my heart, and for the breath that gives me the Life of God.

Breathe •

I breathe in the Spirit of Peace.

I imagine and feel the Spirit of Peace breathing deep, harmonious peace into me.

I breathe it in deeply, wait, and then breathe it out to into my agitations and worries, into my spiritual life, desires, and relationships. I pray that this peace spreads far.

I repeat as desired—breathing, peaceful, in harmony with all....

If I belong to a group seeking peace, we breathe this Spirit together.

Reach Out •

I reach out to those of like mind and heart.

I conclude in thanks, considering two questions. First, if possible, how might I reconnect with the one who brought me great peace? Second, to whom and how do I pass on this exercise? Who urgently needs deep peace now?

Orthopedic Care

Orthopedic care heals muscle, bone, ligaments, and tendons. It is repairs movement. God's field hospital is about healing movement. Illness, disease, and wounds immobilize the body and mind. Even the interior life and spiritual desires can be affected and spiritual progress crippled.

Exercise 41: For the Paralyzed. Joints stiffen, disease spreads, bone fractures, and muscle tears, all disable a life. As do the ligaments of the heart, the muscles of desire, the tears in future goals. The Spirit of Movement can uniquely show the way forward. Exercise 41 is for those who are stuck—physically, emotionally, or spiritually.

Exercise 42: For the Lame. When a leg is fractured, lame, or inflamed, the whole body is unstable and immobilized. The same may be true spiritually, the heart and soul becoming slow, clumsy, and stiff. The Spirit of Agility helps the person to find poise. Exercise 42 is for those who are lame in leg or heart.

Exercise 43: For the Unsteady. Chronically ill people tell themselves the same life story over and over. The need and woundedness seems endless, a weight that bends the spine. Every step a mire, a pitfall of desolation. The Spirit of Steadiness places feet firmly in place. Exercise 43 is for fresh legs and a new song.

Exercise 44: For the Crippled. One does not have to be old to be bent over by the burden of illness. Endless pain ages us. Life wounds can deform us. The Spirit of the spine gives release from the bondage of past burdens and suffering. It offers a fresh dignity and a strong back. Exercise 44 is for "straightening" the spine and "raising" the spirits.

Symptoms of Difficult Movement

Exercise 41. I am paralyzed, hopeless. I am stuck. I feel snap-frozen in my woundedness—petrified by my anxieties. I need to be released from that which has paralyzed me. I desire to move again.

Exercise 42. I am lame, immobilized in body and mind, and having to beg for help. It is humiliating and frustrating. I want to stand on my own two feet. I desire agility and joy.

Exercise 43. I am unsteady, precarious. Every step I take toward health is like walking in a mirey bog. My sickness sucks me into a desolate pit. I desire to steady my feet in a secure place.

Exercise 44. I am bent over, worn down. My old life, my old ways, and even my past strengths are beaten down by my ill health. I am bent over, crippled, even in my soul. I desire to straighten up.

Exercise 41: **For the Paralyzed**

Touch •

I feel arms, wrist, and fingers.

I feel the bones of my arm, upper and lower, wrist and fingers. Holding my upper arm muscle, I flex and lift my arm, I extend it, twist it, rotate the wrist, and clench the fingers, all the while marvelling at the movement in my bones, muscles, and tendons. I push my hand backward, revealing the tendons of each finger.

If well, I see how my body is made for movement. If I have arthritis or injury, I see how devastating restrictions or paralysis can be.

My body is a symbol of my desires and freedom, both practical and spiritual. I consider how many things can immobilize me in life: being trapped by illness, enclosed in distress, paralyzed by despair or powerlessness, stuck with the sudden loss of livelihood, or being bereft of options for the future.

I recall a story of being released from paralysis in a life situation where I was helpless and had lost hope. I remember the person who got me moving again. If praying alone, I hold that memory. If I am praying in a group, we share our stories, feeling touched by the Spirit of Movement.

Desire •

I desire freedom to move.

I slowly and prayerfully read the scripture text below:

> There is a pool, where many invalids lay—blind, lame, and paralyzed. One man was there who had been ill for thirty-eight years. When Jesus saw him lying there and knew that he had been there a long time, he said to him, "Do you want to be made well?" The sick man answered him, "Sir, I have no one to put me into the pool when the water is stirred up (and be healed); and while I am making my way, someone else steps down ahead of me."

> Jesus said to him, "Stand up, take your mat and walk." At once the man was made well, took up his mat and began to walk. (John 5:2–9)

I name all the things that paralyze me.

I ask the Spirit to be made well again, to release me—body and heart—where I am stuck.

Breathe •

I breathe in the Spirit of Movement.

I imagine the Spirit addressing me by name, saying, "Do you want to be healed? Stand up, take up your mat, and walk."

I imagine and feel the Spirit breathing hope, healing, and movement into me. I breathe them in deeply, wait, and then breathe them out into my paralysis, into my chronic suffering, into where I am stuck.

I repeat as desired—breathing, releasing, free....

If I belong to a group seeking the freedom to move, we breathe this Spirit together.

Reach Out •

I reach out to those of like mind and heart.

I conclude in thanks, considering two questions. First, if possible, how might I reconnect with the person who healed me to move again? Second, to whom and how do I pass on this exercise? Who needs help to stand up and move forward now?

Exercise 42: **For the Lame**

Touch •
I feel my feet and ankles.

I feel my foot and ankle. Holding my ankle, I rotate it, bend it up and down, and feel the ligaments moving in the top of my feet and toes. I consider how these bones, ligaments, and tendons allow me to stand walk, reach, leap, and dance.

I walk around slowly feeling that truth. I make a little dance step, savoring the agility and freedom. If well, I wonder at the strength in my ankles, feet, and toes. If I have a sprain or injury, I feel how I am immobilized.

My body is a symbol of my strength, agility, and freedom to go where I wish. This is true physically and spiritually in every desire and action.

I recall a story of mobility when I felt lame, constricted, and powerless by events in body or mind, and a person who helped me to get up and move again. If praying alone, I hold that memory. If I am praying in a group, I share it with them, listening in turn to their stories, feeling touched by the Spirit of Agility.

Desire •
I desire agility.

I slowly and prayerfully read the scripture text below:

> One day Peter and John were going up to the temple at the hour of prayer. And a man lame from birth was being carried in. When he saw Peter and John about to go into the temple, he asked them for alms. Peter looked intently at him, as did John, and said, "Look at us." And he fixed his attention on them, expecting to receive something from the But Peter said, "I have no silver or gold, but what I have I give you; in the name of Jesus Christ of Nazareth, stand up and walk." And he took him by the right hand and raised him up; and immedi-

ately his feet and ankles were made strong. Jumping up, he stood and began to walk, and he entered the temple with them, walking and leaping and praising God. All the people saw him walking and praising God, and they recognized him as the one who used to sit and ask for alms at the Beautiful Gate of the temple; and they were filled with wonder and amazement. (Acts 3:1–10)

I name all the places and events I wish to be able to move in and have a full range of mobility.

I ask the Spirit for the gift of mobility, for agility of heart, mind, and feet.

Breathe •

I breathe in the Spirit of Agility.

I imagine the Spirit addressing me by name, saying, "Stand up. Your feet and ankles are made strong. Dance again with joy, leap with me."

Then I imagine the Spirit breathing the gift of agility, strength, and joy into me. I breathe them in deeply, wait, and then breathe them into my feet and ankles.

I repeat as desired—breathing, strengthening, leaping with agility…

If I belong to a group seeking agility, we breathe this Spirit in and out together.

Reach Out •

I reach out to those of like mind and heart.

I conclude in thanks, considering two questions. First, if possible, how might I reconnect with the person who helped me to move again? Second, to whom and how do I pass on this exercise? Who urgently needs the agility to dance again?

Exercise 43: **For the Unsteady**

Touch •

I feel my knees and legs.

I walk very slowly, small steps in slow motion. As I do, I focus on the muscles in my legs, the movement in my knees, and the automatic balancing of my body that is carried by them. Then sitting, I bend my leg back and forth, feeling the muscles in the upper and lower leg, back and front, and the tendons at the back of my knee.

This is how I stand, walk, and balance. Here is the power to lift, leap, climb, and descend stairs. This is the source of my security when I move. If well, I wonder at this. If I have a torn ligament, bruised muscle, or lame leg, I feel how I am immobilized.

My body is a symbol of my balance, steadiness, and security of movement. This is true physically, in walking, and spiritually, in every interior choice and spiritual journey.

I recall a story of a person who helped me in the depths of chronic injury, or who lifted me up when weak in knee and leg, or who created a secure, safe place for me to steady myself. If praying alone I hold that memory. If I am praying in a group, we share our stories, feeling touched by the Spirit of Steadiness.

Desire •

I desire a firm footing.

I slowly and prayerfully read the scripture text below:

> I waited patiently for the LORD; he inclined to me and heard my cry. He drew me up from the desolate pit, out of the miry bog, and set my feet upon a rock, making my steps secure. He put a new song in my mouth, a song of praise to our God. Many will see and be awed and put their trust in the LORD. (Ps 40)

I name everything that mires my feet, that makes me unsteady in my legs, that drags me into a desolate pit, that brings my interior life to a halt, crying to God for help.

I ask the Spirit for the gift of firm footing, to draw me up from the pit of present circumstances or illness, and to make my steps secure. I ask the Spirit to give me the gift of spiritual safety and steadiness, to put a new song in my mouth.

Breathe •

I breathe in the Spirit of Steadiness.

I imagine the Spirit addressing me, saying, "I hear your cry. I will free you from all the things that hobble your steps and trouble your limping heart. I will set you on firm ground, safe and secure. And I will be with you."

Then I imagine and feel the Spirit breathing the song of steadiness into my legs and knees, and into my weary heart. I breathe it in deeply, wait, and then breathe it out to where I am trapped, bogged down, unsteady and struggling for balance.

I repeat as desired—breathing, steadying, singing a new song....

If I belong to a group seeking steadiness, we breathe this Spirit in and out together.

Reach Out •

I reach out to those of like mind and heart.

I conclude in thanks, considering two questions. First, if possible, how might I reconnect with the one who steadied me when I was bogged down and insecure? Second, to whom and how do I pass on this exercise? Who needs steady feet now?

Exercise 44: **For the Crippled**

Touch •
I feel my hip, spine, and neck.

I bend over and my face only sees the ground. Stretching a little lower, I imagine carrying such a heavy burden that this is the only way to stand. With hands on hip and neck, I imagine my body crippled and arthritic. I walk around slowly, feeling that possibility. Or with swollenness actually crippling my body, I feel the restrictions.

My body is a symbol of my identity. It is how I face the world. It also mirrors my interior life, its wellness or wounds, its memories, and stories. My body, as intimate metaphor, can also illuminate that which cripples my dreams and my spiritual life.

I recall a story of someone who straightened my spine to face the wounds and path before me, or who strengthened the backbone of my spiritual life when I needed it. If praying alone, I hold that memory. If I am praying in a group, I share it with them, listening in turn to their stories, feeling touched by the Spirit of the Spine.

Desire •
I desire to stand up straight.

I slowly and prayerfully read the scripture text below:

> Jesus was teaching in one of the synagogues on the sabbath. And just then there appeared a woman with a spirit that had crippled her for eighteen years. She was bent over and was quite unable to stand up straight. When Jesus saw her, he called her over and said, "Woman, you are set free from your ailment." When he laid his hands on her, immediately she stood up straight and began praising God. To the indignant the leader of the synagogue, Jesus said, "Ought not this woman, a daughter of Abraham whom Satan bound for eighteen long years,

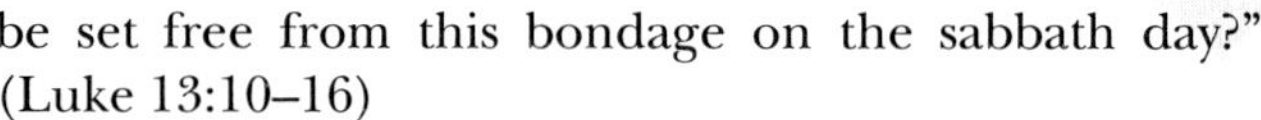
be set free from this bondage on the sabbath day?"
(Luke 13:10–16)

I name all the things that cripple me, all the ailments from which I wish to be free, and all the bondages that bend me over.

I ask the Spirit of the Spine to give me a strong backbone, a way to stand straight again and face the world with peace and hope. I ask for release from the bondage of all the dark, wounded places in me, from all that cripples me.

Breathe •

I breathe in the Spirit of the Spine.

I imagine and feel the Spirit breathing strength and support into my spine. I feel the flow of this gentle Spirit straighten out the spine of my life story, free my shoulders from the weight of sadness, loosen my neck so that I see the horizon again, and align my hips so that I can walk forward smoothly.

I breathe it in deeply, wait, and then breathe it out into my hips, spine, shoulders, and neck.

I repeat as desired—breathing, straightening, healing....

If I belong to a crippled group, we breathe this Spirit in and out together.

Reach Out •

I reach out to those of like mind and heart.

I conclude in thanks, considering two things. First, if possible, how can I reconnect with the one who gave me a backbone to face the wound or illness within me. Second, to whom do I pass on this exercise? Who needs a straight spine to face their world?

Pain Management

Healing is a mystery. Sometimes, even in a field hospital, constant pain is present. It is complex and usually chronic. Pain management is necessary to provide relief so one can enjoy life, even with pain. Hurt or wounds can be deep and widespread, or focused in one place, physically and spiritually.

*Exercise 45: Accepting Tears.** We are made to cry, for we have been created with tear ducts. Sorrow and joy are brother and sister, companions on our life journey. Tears of every kind are welcome in God's field hospital—consoling tears, lamenting tears, cleansing tears, even tears of relief. The Spirit of Tears is a healer. Exercise 45 is for weeping.

*Exercise 46: Seeking Quiet.** The clamor of endless pain deafens the sick to hearing anything else, surrounding them in a bubble of suffering. The rest of their world turns gray, and relationships wither around it. The Spirit of Loving Quiet is like a mother. Exercise 46 offers a cradle of quiet.

Exercise 47: Finding Comfort. Living with trauma or radical loss, one has few companions. Advice from others is often fruitless. Everything that can be done is done. What is needed now is the comfort of a loving, silent presence. The Spirit of Comfort is tender in such companionship. Exercise 47 is for consolation and fresh hope.

Exercise 48: Rekindling Joy. Even when pain is intense, daily, simple joys will balance life and heal. The comfort of a hug, the warmth of the sun, the sight of a friend, the sound of a bird, the scent of a flower, are yours. No one can take your joy away. The Spirit of Joy guarantees this. Exercise 48 is for rekindling joy.

Symptoms of Pain

Exercise 45. My pain withers me inside. I am becoming hard of heart, dry in spirit. My pain has leeched away my tears. My desolation is bitter, my life entombed. How I long to weep.

Exercise 46. My pain is like a roaring lion. I had big plans for my life. Now, my heart prowls the ruins of my suffering. My soul is restless with pain. I need to surrender, to rest in the quiet of God.

Exercise 47. My pain lashes out at friends. Everyone, everything was at fault, including God. I blamed them all for my pain. Yet a voice whispers to me, "Seek the God of comfort and hope." This I will try.

Exercise 48. My pain leaves me joyless. Living in constant pain, my interior life has become a barren field. Reasonably, but foolishly, I stopped feeling the small joys of my life. I want to recover them.

Exercise 45: **Accepting Tears***

Touch •
I touch the heart of tears.

I hold an object that symbolizes healing tears for me.

I recall a story of being consoled of my tears and the support of one who accepted them. If praying alone, I hold that memory. If I am praying in a group, I share it with them, listening in turn to their stories, feeling touched by the Spirit of Tears.

Desire •
I desire free flowing tears.

I consider three things, taking a few minutes to explore each of them. I ask myself:

Where do I accept tears in my life?

Where are tears absent in my life?

What, for me, is the contrary or opposite of tears of consolation?

I ask the Spirit for the gift of healing tears in my pain.

Choose •
I choose the way of tears.

I slowly and prayerfully read the scripture text below:

> When Mary came where Jesus was and saw him, she knelt at his feet and said to him, "Lord, if you had been here, my brother Lazarus would not have died." When Jesus saw her weeping, and the Jews who came with her also weeping, he was greatly disturbed in spirit and deeply moved. He said, "Where have you laid him?" They said to him, "Lord, come and see." Jesus began to weep. Then Jesus, again greatly disturbed, came to the

tomb. He cried with a loud voice, "Lazarus, come out!" The dead man came out. Jesus said, "Unbind him, and let him go." (John 11:32–44)

How do I manage my pain? I choose, in three steps, the direction I wish to take:

I choose to follow the way of consoling tears, drawing me toward the love of God.

I reject the way of spiritual dryness, hard-heartedness, or cynicism, led by a bad spirit.

I turn and walk in the opposite direction, from denial to tears and consolation.

Rest •

I rest in the Spirit of Tears.

I imagine the Spirit saying to me, "Harden not your heart. Weep with those who weep."

I rest awhile, recalling how often Jesus wept. My tears are just as precious.

If I belong to a group seeking healing tears, we rest in this Spirit together.

Reach Out •

I reach out to those of like mind and heart.

I conclude in thanks, considering two questions. First, if possible, how might I reconnect with the one who accepted my tears? Second, to whom and how do I pass on this exercise? Who needs healing tears now?

Exercise 46: **Seeking Quiet***

Touch •
I touch the heart of quiet.

I find and hold an object that symbolizes quiet for me.

I recall a story of being held in silence and quiet, in the most unsettling of times. If praying alone, I hold that memory. If I am praying in a group, I share it with them, listening in turn to their stories, feeling touched by the Spirit of Consoling Quiet.

Desire •
I desire to be quietly held.

I consider three things, taking a few minutes to explore each of them. I ask myself:

Where is loving quiet present in my life?

Where is loving quiet absent from my life?

What, for me, is the contrary or opposite of loving quiet?

I ask for the gift of silent, loving quiet in the arms of God.

Choose •
I choose the way of loving quiet.

I slowly and prayerfully read the scripture text below:

> O LORD, my heart is not lifted up, my eyes are not raised too high; I do not occupy myself with things too great and too marvelous for me. But I have calmed and quieted my soul, like a weaned child with its mother; my soul is like the weaned child that is with me. (Ps 131)

How do I manage my pain? I choose, in three steps, the direction I wish to take:

I choose the quiet way led by the good spirit toward God's love.

I reject the way of disquiet and distress led by a bad spirit.

I turn and walk in the opposite direction from agitation to quiet and restful peace.

Rest •

I rest in the Spirit of Loving Quiet.

I imagine the Spirit saying to me, "Hold yourself in quiet and silence, rest your soul upon my heart."

I am still and silent, resting in the intimacy of the quietening Spirit. I feel loved, protected, and at home.

If I belong to a group seeking loving quiet, we rest in this Spirit together.

Reach Out •

I reach out to those of like mind and heart.

I conclude in thanks, considering two questions. First, if possible, how might I reconnect with the one who held me in quiet and silence? Second, to whom and how do I pass on this exercise? Who needs loving, restful quiet now?

Exercise 47: **Finding Comfort**

Touch •
I touch the heart of comfort.

I hold an object that symbolizes comforting presence for me. I consider how the best comforters seek to be with the other, to awaken a tender heart to live again, to clean the scars, to lessen fears, and to encourage hope. This is the comfort that I also desire.

I recall a story of being comforted when I really needed it. If praying alone, I hold that memory. If I am praying in a group, I share it with them, listening in turn to their stories, feeling touched by the Spirit of Comfort.

Desire •
I desire to be comforted.

I slowly and prayerfully read the scripture text below:

> May our Lord Jesus Christ himself and God our Father, who loved us and through grace gave us eternal comfort and good hope, comfort your hearts and strengthen them in every good work and word. (2 Thess 2:16–17)

I name everything in which I desire to be comforted.

Then I ask the Spirit for deep, enduring comfort, for healing of mind and body, for new life in my tender, bruised heart.

Breathe •
I breathe in the Spirit of Comfort.

I imagine the Spirit addressing me by name, saying, "Blessed are those who mourn, for they will be comforted."

I imagine and feel the Spirit of Comfort breathing strength, hope, companionship, and courage into me. I breathe these gifts in deeply, wait, and then breathe them out to flow through my pain and loneliness.

I repeat as desired—breathing, comforted, strengthened....

If I belong to a group seeking comfort, we breath in this Spirit together.

Reach Out •
I reach out to those of like mind and heart.

I conclude in thanks, considering two questions. First, if possible, how might I reconnect with the person who comforted me? Second, to whom and how do I pass on this exercise? Who urgently needs comfort now?

Exercise 48: **Rekindling Joy**

Touch •
I touch the heart of joy.

I ring a small bell. I listen to its sensual sound, carried in the air. I consider how the unseen Spirit is like the unseen sound. I ponder how, in the time of my need, that Spirit could ring with new life in me. I ring, feeling the touch of the Spirit. I repeat....

I recall a story of someone giving me great joy in a dark and bleak time. If praying alone, I hold that memory. If I am praying in a group, I share it with them, listening in turn to their stories, feeling touched by the Spirit of Joy.

Desire •
I desire simple joys.

I slowly and prayerfully read the scripture text below:

> Very truly, I tell you, you will weep and mourn, but the world will rejoice; you will have pain, but your pain will turn into joy. When a woman is in labour, she has pain, because her hour has come. But when her child is born, she no longer remembers the anguish because of the joy of having brought a human being into the world. So you have pain now; but I will see you again, and your hearts will rejoice, and no one will take your joy from you. On that day you will ask nothing of me. Very truly, I tell you, if you ask anything of the Father in my name, he will give it to you. Until now you have not asked for anything in my name. Ask and you will receive, so that your joy may be complete. (John 16:20–24)

I name all the small joys in my life, and all the great joys that are to come.

I ask the Spirit for a living, stirring joy in painful or unhappy times.

Breathe •

I breathe in the Spirit of Joy.

I imagine the Spirit addressing me by name, saying, "Listen, I really do enjoy you. May your joy be complete in me."

Then I imagine and feel the Spirit breathing joy and happiness into me. I breathe them in deeply, wait, and then breathe them out into my life and relationships, into the sad, joyless places.

I repeat as desired—breathing, joyful, happy....

If I belong to a group seeking joy, we breathe in this Spirit together.

Reach Out •

I reach out to those of like mind and heart.

I conclude in thanks, considering two questions. First, if possible, how might I reconnect with the person who filled me with joy in dark times? Second, to whom and how do I pass on this exercise? Who urgently needs joy now?

V

Recovery Care

Physical Therapy

Physical therapy is an exercise-based approach to physiotherapy. It restores health, mobility, and well-being. Like a spiritual exercise, physical therapy involves you in your own healing while working with the healer. Rehabilitation heals physical injuries. God's field hospital also treats spiritual aches and pains.

Exercise 49: Reverence. The beginning of healing body and spirit is to treat both with respect and reverence, no matter how wounded, diseased, seemingly ugly, or powerless. The Spirit of Reverence welcomes all with honor. Exercise 49 is for tender reverence of body and soul.

Exercise 50: Self-Care. A good self-image is often one of the first causalities of chronic illness if the image was based on productivity for identity. False self-images can lead to anger, denial, and being hard on the wounded self. The Spirit of Self-Care reverses this. Exercise 50 is for those who want to enjoy themselves as is.

Exercise 51: Rest. Rest and recreation are essential for balancing work and life. Furthermore, every healing path begins with rest. Often the best physical therapy is simply to stop for a while. The Spirit of Rest helps when the inner taskmaster presses too hard. Exercise 51 is for those desiring refreshment of body and spirit.

*Exercise 52: Delight.** Our sense of delight is a powerful expression of humanity. A life story will hold many personal delights—great and small. Being wounded or sick can turn one away from delightful experiences, people, and nature. The Spirit of Delight is a surprising healer and remedy. Exercise 52 is for becoming delightful.

Symptoms Needing Physical Therapy

Exercise 49. I am treated harshly. I have lost my power since being ill. People disregard me and even scorn my vulnerability as being over dramatic. This belittles me. I desire reverence.

Exercise 50. I keep beating myself up. I am so angry with myself. I despise how useless I have become. The worst part of being wounded is how I put myself down. I need to begin some self-care.

Exercise 51. I am totally exhausted. I have no energy left. My sickness with the burdens of my life has piled stress upon stress. Nothing prepared me for this. I need to stop. I desire real daily rest.

Exercise 52. I am living in darkness. My life has become desperately gray. I am afraid of the miseries that plague my days. But should illness be constantly bleak? I want to feel delight.

Exercise 49: **Reverence**

Touch •
I touch the heart of reverence.

I hold a gesture of humble reverence. Reverence is a feeling or attitude of deep respect tinged with awe. It can also mean veneration, esteem, and honor. One can hold a newborn child with reverence, esteem the sick, respect prisoners, and honor the tortured, because God reverences them. I can even be reverent to myself because of God's mutual love for me. I consider the healing power of reverence.

I recall a story of someone treating me with tender, loving reverence when I felt unloved and rejected. If praying alone, I hold that memory. If I am praying in a group, we listen in turn to our stories, feeling touched by the Spirit of Reverence.

Desire •
I desire to be reverenced.

I slowly and prayerfully read the scripture text below:

> Let mutual love continue. Do not neglect to show hospitality to strangers, for by doing that some have entertained angels without knowing it. Remember those who are in prison, as though you were in prison with them; those who are being tortured, as though you yourselves were being tortured. So we can say with confidence, "The Lord is my helper; I will not be afraid. What can anyone do to me?" (Heb 13:1–4, 6)

I name the relationships where I am treated with disrespect, even with contempt. I remember the experiences that dehumanized me.

I ask the Spirit for a healing reverence in my relationships.

Breathe •

I breathe in the Spirit of Reverence.

I imagine the Spirit addressing me by name, saying, "Do not be afraid. I love you and reverence you. Learn to reverence yourself."

I imagine the Spirit of Reverence breathing into me awe, respect, and humility. I breathe in deeply, pause, and then breathe them out into my relationships and life situations where there is disrespect, dismissal, violence, contempt, or shame.

I repeat as desired—breathing, reverenced, humble....

If I belong to a group needing reverence, we breathe this Spirit in and out together.

Reach Out •

I reach out to those of like mind and heart.

I conclude in thanks, considering two questions. First, if possible, how might I reconnect with the person who reverenced me? Second, to whom and how do I pass on this exercise? Who urgently needs reverence now?

Exercise 50: **Self-Care**

Touch •

I touch the heart of self-care.

I make a list of seven activities, places, or people that refresh me. I fold and hold it as a symbol of self-care. As I do, I consider the family of gifts to which self-care belongs: self-esteem, self-confidence, and self-control. This is a delightful path.

I recall a story of someone who showed me how to care for myself when I was overburdened and exhausted. If praying alone, I hold that memory. If I am praying in a group, we share our stories in turn, feeling touched by the Spirit of Self-Care.

Desire •

I desire to care for myself.

I slowly and prayerfully read the scripture text below:

> My child, treat yourself well, according to your means, and present worthy offerings to the Lord. Remember that death does not tarry, and the decree of Hades has not been shown to you. Do good to friends before you die and reach out and give to them as much as you can. Do not deprive yourself of a day's enjoyment; do not let your share of desired good pass by you. (Sir 14:11–14)

I name all the things I wish to enjoy and care for within me.

I ask the spirit for the gifts of greater self-care, self-love, and enjoyment of each day, and for freedom from my own or others' expectations and demands.

Breathe •

I breathe in the Spirit of Self-Care.

I imagine the Spirit breathing esteem, self-love, and self-care.

I breathe them in deeply, wait, and then breathe them out into my life, my self-image, and my self-confidence.

I repeat as desired—breathing, self-caring, treating myself well....

If I belong to a group needing self-care, we breathe this Spirit in and out together.

Reach Out •

I reach out to those of like mind and heart.

I conclude in thanks, considering two questions. First, if possible, how might I make contact and reconnect with the one who showed me how to care for myself? Second, to whom and how do I pass on this exercise? Who needs self-care now?

Exercise 51: **Rest**

Touch •
I touch the heart of rest and recreation.

I hold a cup or glass of a relaxing drink, like a cup of tea or glass of wine. This can be a symbol of my need to rest.

I recall a story of someone who helped me to rest when I was too tired to see my need of it. If praying alone, I hold that memory. If I am praying in a group, I share it with them, feeling touched by the Spirit of Rest.

Desire •
I desire to rest.

I slowly and prayerfully read the scripture text below:

> The apostles gathered around Jesus and told him all that they had done and taught. He said, "Come away to a deserted place all by yourselves and rest a while." For many were coming and going, and they had no leisure even to eat. So they went away in the boat to a deserted place by themselves. (Mark 6:30–32)

I name all the ways I would like to rest.

I ask the Spirit of rest for the twin gifts of rest and leisure, to recharge myself for the long healing journey ahead, and to savor precious moments with family, friends, and even nature.

Rest •

I breathe in the Spirit of Rest.

I imagine and feel the Spirit of Rest breathing refreshing rest into me. I am re-created.

I breathe it in deeply, wait, and then breathe it out through my need, especially when I am suffering from illness and in need of healing, trapped by overwork or overcommitment, or just feeling plain exhaustion.

I repeat as desired—breathing, resting, renewing....

If I belong to a group needing rest, we breathe this Spirit in and out together.

Reach Out •

I reach out to those of like mind and heart.

I conclude in thanks, considering two questions. First, if possible, how might I make contact and reconnect with the one who convinced me to rest? Second, to whom and how do I pass on this exercise? Who urgently needs healing rest now?

Exercise 52: **Delight***

Touch •
I touch the heart of delight.

I find an object that symbolizes delight for me. I hold it remembering the times I have been delighted, and I consider how natural a delighted heart is for our humanity.

I recall a story of someone who has delighted me. If praying alone, I hold that memory. If I am praying in a group, I share it with them, listening in turn to their stories, feeling touched by the Spirit of Delight.

Desire •
I desire to be delightful.

I consider three things, taking a few minutes to explore each. I ask myself:

Where is delight present in my life?

Where is delight absent in my life?

What, for me, is the contrary or opposite of delight?

I ask the Spirit for the gift of physical and spiritual delight.

Choose •
Today, I choose the way of delight.

I slowly and prayerfully read the scripture text below:

> Trust in the LORD, and do good; so you will live in the land, and enjoy security. Take delight in the LORD, and he will give you the desires of your heart. Commit your way to the LORD; trust in him, and he will act. He will make your vindication shine like the light, and the justice of your cause like the noonday. Be still before the LORD and wait patiently for him. (Ps 37)

I choose, in three thoughtful steps, the direction I wish to take:

I choose to follow the way of delight, guided by the good spirit, toward greater Light.

I reject the way of dismay, of being harried by the bad spirit into greater darkness.

I turn and walk in the opposite direction from discontent to delight and deep peace.

Rest •

I rest in the Spirit of Delight.

I imagine the Spirit addressing me, saying, "You are my delight. I will never desert you."

I rest for a time—now and reflectively throughout the whole day—drinking from the river of the Spirit's delights. I become delightful.

If I belong to a group seeking delight, we rest in this Spirit together.

Reach Out •

I reach out to those of like mind and heart.

I conclude in thanks, considering two questions. First, if possible, how might I make contact and reconnect with the one who delighted me? Second, to whom and how do I pass on this exercise? Who urgently needs delight now?

Rehabilitation

Rehabilitation is an integral part of convalescence. It is the process of restoring a person's ability to live as normally as possible after a disabling injury or illness. God's field hospital offers exercises to learn or relearn healing habits for daily life and for making spiritual as well as physical progress.

Exercise 53: Daily Gratitude. This exercise is built on the Ignatian Awareness Examen, a short prayer to name the good things and God's presence in the day. Daily gratitude is inherently healing. It balances tough times. The Spirit of Gratitude changes how everything looks. Exercise 53 is for the habit of healing thankfulness.

Exercise 54: Daily Resilience. Resilience is the ability to adjust to or recover readily from illness, adversity, or major life changes, including being spiritually stretched or compressed to breaking point. Healing often includes relapses as it moves forward. The Spirit of Resilience adds flexibility to life. Exercise 54 is for bouncing back.

*Exercise 55: Daily Progress.** Healing is a journey not an event; it is growth not an endpoint. Paradoxically, people who come through illness and healing become more whole not less. God's field hospital is a place to move from good to better, both physically and spiritually. The Spirit of Progress leads to healing. Exercise 55 is for moving forward.

Exercise 56: Daily Dreams. Without dreams we dry up, a husk of who we could be. Without imagining wild and wonderful things, we fall into the coma of the past. Without spiritual visions, we live a half-life. Without all these, we will not fully heal. The Spirit of Dreams rehabilitates audacious imagination. Exercise 56 is for dreamers.

Symptoms Needing Rehabilitation

Exercise 53. My day seems endlessly bleak. Every hour, I battle against pain and relapse. Every day feels miserable. Every week a repeat of the last. I have lost sight of the good things. I need gratitude.

Exercise 54. I have had it! My ill health has knocked me over so many times, I have lost the heart to get up again. I feel beaten down and am stretched to breaking point. I need the gift of resilience.

Exercise 55. My life is going nowhere. I gave my body time to heal. I gave my spirit time to adjust, but my ill health keeps crossing those lines. I need progress in body and spirit.

Exercise 56. I have lost all my dreams. I used to dream of all the great and wonderful things I would do, the person I would become, but my long ill health shattered them. I hope to dream again.

Exercise 53: **Daily Gratitude**

Touch •
I touch the heart of gratitude.

I write a letter of gratitude to God. I review my last week, hour by hour, day by day, writing down everything, large and small, for which I feel grateful. This letter is a good symbol of gratitude. I consider how the Spirit works through me in these happy events.

I recall a story of someone who expressed their gratitude to me. If praying alone, I hold that memory. If I am praying in a group, I share it with them, listening in turn to their stories, feeling touched by the Spirit of Gratitude.

Desire •
I desire daily gratitude.

I slowly and prayerfully read the scripture text below:

> Let the peace of Christ rule in your hearts. And be thankful. Let the word of Christ dwell in you richly; teach and admonish one another in all wisdom; and with gratitude in your hearts sing psalms, hymns, and spiritual songs to God. And whatever you do, in word or deed, do everything in the name of the Lord Jesus, giving thanks to God the Father through him. (Col 3:15–17)

I name all the things for which I am grateful.

I consider the hard places of my illness and healing and imagine God at work there.

I ask the Spirit for a grateful heart, to see the good and enriching things in my day. I choose not to dwell on the ailments, losses, disappointments, or resentments—no matter how understandable.

Breathe •

I breathe in the Spirit of Gratitude.

I imagine the Spirit of Gratitude breathing into me an awareness of today's gifts.

I breathe it in deeply, wait, and then breathe it out into my tomorrow.

I repeat as desired—breathing, grateful, peaceful....

If I belong to a grateful group, we breathe this Spirit together.

Reach Out •

I reach out to those of like mind and heart.

I conclude in thanks, considering two questions. First, if possible, how might I make contact and reconnect with the one who was grateful for me? Second, to whom and how do I pass on this exercise? Who urgently needs to be filled with gratitude?

Exercise 54: **Daily Resilience**

Touch •

I touch the heart of resilience.

I take a thin bamboo rod, or pliant branch, slowly bend it, and then watch and feel how it gives and then springs back. I repeat, reflecting on how its flexible, yielding strength prevents it from breaking.

I recall a story of someone who taught and showed me how to be resilient. If praying alone I hold that memory. If I am praying in a group, I share it with them, listening in turn to their stories, feeling touched by the Spirit of Resilience.

Desire •

I desire daily resilience.

I slowly and prayerfully read the scripture text below:

> As servants of God, we have commended ourselves in every way: through great endurance, in afflictions, hardships, calamities, beatings, imprisonments, riots, labours, sleepless nights, hunger; by purity, knowledge, patience, kindness, holiness of spirit, genuine love, truthful speech, and the power of God; in honour and dishonour, in ill repute and good repute. We are treated as imposters, and yet are true; as unknown, and yet are well known; as dying, and see—we are alive; as punished, and yet not killed; as sorrowful, yet always rejoicing; as poor, yet making many rich; as having nothing, and yet possessing everything. (2 Cor 6:3–6)

I name all the experiences in which I wish to show resilience.

I ask the Spirit for the gift of resilience, to endure suffering, to bend with the stormy winds, becoming strong in weakness, especially in the face of an unknown future.

Breathe •

I breathe in the Spirit of Resilience.

I imagine the Spirit addressing me by name, saying, "I am the God of all consolation. My power will be with you in all the ups and downs of your life."

I imagine and feel the Spirit breathing supple resilience into me. I breathe it in deeply and then breathe it out into my bruised heart, straining muscles and flagging emotions.

I repeat as desired—breathing, resilient, moving forward....

If I belong to a group seeking resilience, we breathe this Spirit together.

Reach Out •

I reach out to those of like mind and heart.

I conclude in thanks, considering two questions. First, if possible, how might I reconnect with the person who increased my resilience? Second, to whom and how do I pass on this exercise? Who urgently needs resilience now.

Exercise 55: **Daily Progress***

Touch •

I touch the heart of moving forward freely.

I find and hold an object that symbolizes for me the easing or taking away of illusory obstacles, so that I can move forward in service. Like my body and my breath, the Spirit who is the Breath of God needs clear airways to give me life.

I recall a story of false obstacles melting away to my good actions when I wanted to move forward. If praying alone, I hold that memory. If am praying in a group, I share it with them, feeling touched by the Spirit of Progress.

Desire •

I desire daily progress.

I consider three things, taking a few minutes exploring each. I ask myself:

> Where is progress, the gift to do greater good, present in my life?
>
> Where is such progress absent in my life?
>
> What, for me, is the contrary or opposite of spiritual progress?

I ask the Spirit that seemingly insurmountable mountains be removed from my heart and imagination, so that I may move forward peacefully, healed in every way.

Choose •

I choose the way of progress.

I slowly and prayerfully read the scripture text below:

> It shall be said, "Build up, build up, prepare the way, remove every obstruction from my people's way." For thus says the high and lofty one who inhabits eternity,

whose name is Holy: "I dwell in the high and holy place, and also with those who are contrite and humble in spirit, to revive the spirit of the humble, and to revive the heart of the contrite. I have seen their ways, but I will heal them; I will lead them and repay them with comfort. Peace, peace, to the far and the near, says the LORD; and I will heal them." (Isa 57:14–19)

I choose, in three thoughtful steps, the direction I wish to take:

I choose the open way, led by the good Spirit, who removes obstacles to love.

I reject the spurious obstacles, imagined, or feared, placed in my path by the bad spirit.

I turn and walk in the opposite direction moving forward from dismay to freedom.

Rest •

I rest in the Spirit of Progress.

I imagine the Spirit of Progress saying, "I will remove every obstacle in your way. Nothing will separate you from my love."

I rest for a while—now and reflectively through the whole day—in the Spirit of Progress who dispels my fears, false reasoning, and obstacles to healing.

If I belong to a group seeking spiritual progress, we rest in this Spirit together.

Reach Out •

I reach out to those of like mind and heart.

I conclude in thanks, considering two questions. First, if possible, how might I make contact and reconnect with the one who freed me? Second, to whom and how do I pass on this exercise? Who urgently needs freeing from spurious obstacles now?

Exercise 56: **Daily Dreams**

Touch •
I touch the heart of dreams.

I find an object that symbolizes a dream I have. Holding it with reverence and humility, I open myself to the Spirit of Dreams. I consider that God dreams in us, and we in God.

I recall a story of the first time I began to dream of a great change or gift in my life when I needed it. If praying alone, I hold that memory. If I am praying in a group, I share it with them, listening in turn to their stories, feeling touched by the Spirit of Dreams.

Desire •
I desire daily dreaming.

I slowly and prayerfully read the scripture text below:

> On the day of Pentecost, the disciples were all together in one place. And suddenly from heaven there came a sound like the rush of a violent wind, and it filled the entire house where they were sitting. Divided tongues, as of fire, appeared among them, and a tongue rested on each of them. All of them were filled with the Holy Spirit and began to speak in other languages, as the Spirit gave them ability. Peter addressed the crowds, "Men of Judea and all who live in Jerusalem, let this be known to you, and listen to what I say, this is what was spoken through the prophet Joel: 'In the last days it will be, God declares, that I will pour out my Spirit upon all flesh, and your sons and your daughters shall prophesy, and your young men shall see visions, and your old men shall dream dreams.'" (Acts 2:14–18)

I name all the important aspects of my dreams and my vision for the future.

I ask the Spirit for help to realize these dreams, and to be healed and transformed by them.

Breathe •

I breathe in the Spirit of Dreams.

I imagine the Spirit of Dreams addressing me by name, saying, "Watch for the new thing that I am going to do for you. See, it is happening already."

I imagine the Spirit of Dreams breathing into me audacity, creativity, and excitement. I breathe them in deeply, pause, and then breathe them out into my dreams.

I repeat as desired—breathing, dreaming, audacious....

If I belong to a group ready to dream, we breathe in this Spirit together.

Reach Out •

I reach out to those of like mind and heart.

I conclude in thanks, considering two questions. First, if possible, how might I make contact and reconnect with the one who encouraged my dream? Second, to whom and how do I pass on this exercise? Who urgently needs a transforming dream?

Recovery Ward

The God of the field hospital heals in extravagant ways. Supremely generous, this God invites the ill and wounded to have second helpings of a healing grace, to try more healing remedies, and to receive more gifts of faith, hope, and love. This is the enduring, far-sighted, greater, humbler part of true recovery.

*Exercise 57: Enduring Faith.** Any kind of endurance is hard won. An enduring faith of healers in the healing process and an ungrudging God matures us. Paradoxically, we are made more complete in the end after having been broken by ill health. The Spirit of Enduring Faith brings joy and wisdom. Exercise 57 is for enduring faith.

*Exercise 58: Far-Sighted Hope.** In God's field hospital, hope is not a "fingers-crossed" gamble; you already know that the dice has no numbers on it. This hope comes when you utterly lose your former hopes. Only then, filled with the Spirit of Far-Sighted Hope will you know true hope. Exercise 58 is for an eagle-eyed spiritual hope.

*Exercise 59: Greater Love.** Sudden wounds are a surprise that bends us over in pain. Chronic ill health spirals us into darkness, but if we persist, the journey through sickness and healing will give us a deeper capacity to love. The Spirit of Greater Love is a superb healer. Exercise 59 is for lovers.

Exercise 60: Humble Service. The healing process through small and humble service is the least known way—for who imagines that the one who is most wounded or ill, who has the least in resources, will be healed by service to others. The Spirit of Humble Service works through simple gifts, humbly offered. Exercise 60 is for wounded givers.

Symptoms Needing Recovery

Exercise 57. My faith is stretched. I do not know what I believe anymore. Is God even listening? My lack of health is a trial I am barely surviving. I need a steadying faith.

Exercise 58. My hopes have shriveled. I keep hoping and waiting for healing, endlessly. Now my hope is exhausted, short-sighted. I need a far-sighted hope.

Exercise 59. My love is dried up. I took my loving heart for granted, but my illness has leeched away past affections and left my heart weary. I seek the greater love born of suffering.

Exercise 60. I have no time for anyone else. I have few resources. I have little energy. I have withdrawn from people. Yet I do have some healing wisdom to offer people, small gifts. I desire to share them.

Exercise 57: **Enduring Faith***

Touch •

I touch the heart of an enduring faith.

I find and hold an object that symbolizes enduring, mature faith for me.

I recall a story of a person helping me to endure with faith when I needed it.

If praying alone, I hold that memory. If I am praying in a group, I share it with them, listening in turn to their stories, feeling touched by the Spirit of Enduring Faith.

Desire •

I desire enduring faith.

I consider three things, taking a few minutes to explore each of them. I ask myself:

Where has my faith endured in my life?

Where has my faith been tossed about in the winds of my woundedness?

What, for me, is the contrary or opposite of enduring faith?

I ask the Spirit for a joyful, enduring, mature faith, lacking nothing.

Choose •

Today, I choose the way of enduring faith.

I slowly and prayerfully read the scripture text below:

> My brothers and sisters, whenever you face trials of any kind, consider it nothing but joy, because you know that the testing of your faith produces endurance; and let endurance have its full effect, so that you may be mature

and complete, lacking in nothing. If any of you is lacking in wisdom, ask God, who gives to all generously and ungrudgingly, and it will be given you. (Jas 1:2–5)

I choose, in three thoughtful steps, the direction I wish to take:

I choose the faithful way, led by enduring faith and the good Spirit, to God's love.

I reject the doubting way, double-minded and unstable, amplified by a bad spirit.

I walk toward the generous God from belief to enduring faith and wisdom.

Rest •

I rest in the Spirit of Enduring Faith.

I imagine the Spirit of Enduring Faith addressing me by name, saying, "In your endurance of faith, you will be made complete, lacking in nothing."

I rest in the ungrudging generosity of the Spirit of Enduring Faith. I feel my faith grow, deepen, becoming more complete and wiser.

If I belong to a group seeking to have enduring faith, we rest in this Spirit together.

Reach Out •

I reach out to those of like mind and heart.

I conclude in thanks, considering two questions. First, if possible, how might I make contact and reconnect with the one who gave me enduring faith? Second, to whom and how do I pass on this exercise? Who urgently needs enduring faith now?

Exercise 58: **Far-Sighted Hope***

Touch •
I touch the heart of greater hope.

I find and hold an object that symbolizes greater hope for me. I consider how in my woundedness I have let go of the small hopes I used to carry. Now, after scaling the cliffs of ill health and healing, I see a distant horizon and new possibilities with keen eyes.

I recall a story of receiving hope from a person when I was utterly hopeless. If praying alone, I hold that memory. If I am praying in a group, I share it with them, listening in turn to their stories, feeling touched by the Spirit of Far-Sighted Hope.

Desire •
I desire a far-sighted hope.

I consider three things, taking a few minutes to explore each of them. I ask myself:

Where is hope increasing in my life? Where is it far-sighted?

Where is hope decreasing in my life?

What, for me, is the contrary or opposite of hope?

I ask the Spirit for a far-sighted hope, especially when I feel hope's absence the most. Looking to the horizon of my life, I express what I most hope for now.

Choose •
Today, I choose the way of far-sighted hope.

I slowly and prayerfully read the scripture text below:

> If you direct your heart rightly, you will stretch out your hands toward God. If iniquity is in your hand, put it far away, and do not let wickedness reside in your tents.

Surely then you will lift up your face without blemish; you will be secure, and will not fear. You will forget your misery; you will remember it as waters that have passed away. And your life will be brighter than the noonday; its darkness will be like the morning. And you will have confidence because there is hope. (Job 11:13–18)

I choose, in three thoughtful steps, the direction I wish to take:

I choose the hopeful way, led by keen sight and the good Spirit, toward God's love.

I reject the despairing way, a myopic bleak future, darkened by a bad spirit.

I turn and walk in the opposite direction from darkness to far-sighted, new hope.

Rest •

I rest in the Spirit of Far-Sighted Hope.

I imagine the Spirit addressing me, "Do not be afraid, you are secure in me. Hope for greater things, larger possibilities, new life."

I rest a while in the bright, dawning light of the Spirit. I feel secure and confident.

If I belong to a group seeking to have discerning hope, we rest in this Spirit together.

Reach Out •

I reach out to those of like mind and heart.

I conclude in thanks, considering two questions. First, if possible, how might I make contact and reconnect with the one who gave me hope? Second, to whom and how do I pass on this exercise? Who urgently needs greater hope now?

Exercise 59: **Greater Love***

Touch •
I touch the heart of increasing love.

I hold an object that symbolizes the feeling of my increasing love for God.

I recall a story of receiving greater love when I needed it. If praying alone, I hold that memory. If I am praying in a group, I share it with them, listening in turn to their stories, feeling touched by the Spirit of Greater Love.

Desire •
I desire greater love.

I consider three things, taking a few minutes to explore each of them. I ask myself:

Where do I feel love increasing in my life?

Where do I feel love decreasing in my life?

What, for me, is the contrary or opposite of love?

I ask the Spirit for a greater love, to build me up in this time of recovery, to heal me when I move out, and to love others as I have been loved.

Choose •
Today, I choose the way of greater love.

I slowly and prayerfully read the scripture text below:

> If I have all faith, to remove mountains, but do not have love, I am nothing. Love is patient; love is kind; love is not envious or boastful or arrogant or rude. It does not insist on its own way; it is not irritable or resentful; it does not rejoice in wrongdoing but rejoices in the truth. It bears all things, believes all things, hopes all

things, endures all things. When I was a child, I spoke like a child, I thought like a child, I reasoned like a child; when I became an adult, I put an end to childish ways. And now faith, hope, and love abide, these three; and the greatest of these is love. (1 Cor 13:2–3, 4–7, 11–13)

I choose, in three thoughtful steps, the direction I wish to take:

I choose the loving way, led by greater love and the good Spirit, toward God's love.

I reject the loveless, cold, isolated, and selfish way, dragged down by the bad spirit.

I walk toward the gift and the Giver from affection to greater love and peace in God.

Rest •

I rest in the Spirit of Greater Love.

I imagine the Spirit addressing me by name, saying, "Love others, both friends and strangers, as I have loved you."

So, I rest—now and reflectively through the whole day—in the Spirit's loving and healing intimacy. I feel love grow and thrive within me.

If I belong to a group seeking to have greater love, we rest in this Spirit together.

Reach Out •

I reach out to those of like mind and heart.

I conclude in thanks, considering two questions. First, if possible, how might I make contact and reconnect with the one who showed me greater love. Second, to whom and how do I pass on this exercise? Who urgently needs greater love now?

Exercise 60: **Humbler Service**

Touch •
I touch the heart of service.

I hold my body in a humble bow, a symbol of surrender, reverence, and service. Holding this gesture, I consider whom I serve now, and whom I would like to serve. I reflect on the joy that service gives to my life. I open myself to the Spirit of Humble Service.

I recall a story of humble service and a person who invited me to serve. If praying alone, I hold that memory. If I am praying in a group, I share it with them, listening in turn to their stories, feeling touched by the Spirit of Humble Service.

Desire •
I desire humbler service.

I slowly and prayerfully read the scripture text below:

> Now there are varieties of gifts, but the same Spirit; and there are varieties of services, but the same Lord; and there are varieties of activities, but it is the same God who activates all of them in everyone. To each is given the manifestation of the Spirit for the common good. (1 Cor 12:4)

I name all those I wish to serve.
I ask the Spirit for a heart filled with humble service.

Breathe •

I breathe in the Spirit of Humble Service.

I imagine the Spirit addressing me by name, saying, "With my fire in your heart, my gifts in your arms, and my love in your feet, reach out to help others."

I imagine the Spirit breathing generous service into me. I breathe it in deeply, wait, and then breathe it out through my desire to leave my comfort zone and serve.

I repeat as desired—breathing, healed, ready to serve....

If I belong to a group seeking humbler service, we breathe in this Spirit together.

Reach Out •

I reach out to those of like mind and heart.

I conclude in thanks, considering two questions. First, if possible, how might I reconnect with the person who called me to serve others? Second, to whom and how do I pass on this exercise? How can I serve those in greater need?

Bibliography

Borghesi, Massimo. *Catholic Discordance: Neoconservatism vs. the Field Hospital Church of Pope Francis*. Translated by Barry Hudock. Collegeville, MN: Liturgical Press Academic, 2021.

Brigham, Erin. *Church as Field Hospital: Toward an Ecclesiology of Sanctuary*. Collegeville, MN: Liturgical Press, 2022. Kindle.

Cavanaugh, William T. *Field Hospital: The Church's Engagement with a Wounded World*. Grand Rapids, MI: William B. Eerdmans Publishing, 2016.

Guile, Alan, and Jim McManus, CSsR. *Healing Wounds in the Field Hospital of the Church*. London: Gracewing Publishing, 2017.

Hansen, Michael, SJ. *The First Spiritual Exercises*. Notre Dame, IN: Ave Maria Press, 2013.

———. *The Gospels for Prayer*. Melbourne: John Garratt Publishing, 2009.

Ignatius of Loyola. *Personal Writings: Reminiscences, Spiritual Diary, Select Letters Including the Text of the Spiritual Exercises*. Translated by Joseph A. Munitiz, SJ, and Philip Endean, SJ. London: Penguin Books,1996.

Ivereigh, Austen. *Wounded Shepherd: Pope Francis and His Struggle to Convert the Catholic Church*. New York: Henry Holt, 2019.

Pope Francis. *A Big Heart Open to God*. New York: HarperOne, 2013.

———. *Fratelli Tutti: On Fraternity and Social Friendship*. Our Sunday Visitor, 2020. Kindle.

———. *The Joy of the Gospel: Evangelii Gaudium*. United States Conference of Catholic Bishops, 2013.

———. *The Name of God Is Mercy: A Conversation with Andrea Tornielli*. Translated by Oonagh Stransky. New York: Random House, 2017. Kindle.

Index of Symptoms

The following is a list of symptoms one might have in coming to God's field hospital. Found at the head of each department opposite the introductory descriptions, they are an excellent way to go to the heart of what one needs now and to choose the appropriate exercise in discerning and treating the deeper issue.